Duffy

Ancestors

Compiled by Geoff Duffy

Ancestors of Dan Duffy

Larry Dan Duffy

b: 22 Jun 1939
Centralia, Lewis,
Washington
m: 05 Aug 1967
Centralia,
Washington
d:

Clinton Rex Duffy

b: 05 Feb 1917
Centralia, Lewis,
Washington
m: 1938 Tacoma,
Pierce, Washington
d: Sep 1988 Chula
Vista, San Diego,
California

Violet Oresta Yoakum

b: 10 Apr 1919
Tenino, Thurston,
Washington
d: 23 Dec 1990
Centralia, Lewis,
Washington

Lloyd Franklin Duffy

b: 29 Sep 1889
Washington
m: 26 Jun 1916
Lewis, Washington
d: 23 May 1930
Centralia, Lewis,
Washington

 **2**

Eunice Anderson

b: Nov 1897
Washington
d: 23 May 1930
Centralia, Lewis,
Washington

3

Thomas Ralph Yoakum

b: 03 Jun 1879
Mount Pleasant,
Henry, Iowa
m: 1905
d: 16 Apr 1942
Centralia, Lewis,
Washington

 **4**

Margaret Lyons MacDonald

b: 11 Jan 1889
Tatamagouche,
Colchester, Nova
Scotia, Canada
d: 19 May 1980
Centralia, Lewis,
Washington

5

Lloyd Franklin Duffy

b: 29 Sep 1889
Washington
m: 26 Jun 1916
Lewis, Washington
d: 23 May 1930
Centralia, Lewis,
Washington

Horatio Joseph Duffy

b: 19 Jun 1851
Wheeling, Marshall
County, West
Virginia
m: 03 Nov 1878
Lewis, Washington
d: 08 Jan 1927
Spokane,
Washington

Norah Ida Bell Long

b: Jun 1861 Marion,
Henry, Iowa
d: 05 Jan 1917
Lewis Washington

Bernard Andrew Duffy

b: Aug 1805
Donegal, Ireland
m: 1833
Pennsylvania
d: 08 Sep 1869
St.Louis, St. Louis
Missouri

Elizabeth "Ely" Hess

b: 05 Aug 1812
Westmoreland
County,
Pennsylvania
d: 22 Feb 1907
Macon County,
Missouri

6 

William Henry Long

b: 25 Nov 1824
Franklin, Ohio
m:
d: 10 Feb 1892
Chehalis, Lewis,
Washington

7

Socelia Wirick

b: 28 Mar 1827
Lebanon,
Pennsylvania
d: 12 Dec 1868
Henry County,
Iowa

8

1

9

Charles Perry Anderson

b: 24 Mar 1825 Kentucky
m: 16 Mar 1851 Nodaway, Missouri
d: 23 Sep 1905 Centralia, Lewis, Washington

Mary Ann Cahoon

b: 14 Dec 1829 Ohio
d: 01 Jun 1902 Centralia, Lewis, Washington

George Washington Anderson

b: 24 Feb 1861 Portland, Multnomah, Oregon
m: 1896
d: 04 Jan 1946 Lewis County, Washington

Eunice Anderson

b: Nov 1897 Washington
m: 26 Jun 1916 Lewis, Washington
d: 23 May 1930 Centralia, Lewis, Washington

1

Amelia Alice Sewall

b: Mar 1871 Washington
d: 06 Jan 1941 Lewis

Chris Sewall

b: 25 Dec 1828 Prussia
m:
d: 25 Nov 1895 Centralia, Lewis, Washington

Rosa

b: 23 Mar 1829 Prussia
d: 28 Oct 1911 Centralia, Lewis, Washington

Edward C. Yoakum

10

b: 02 Mar 1814 Claiborne
County, Tennessee
m: 04 Jul 1839 Muscatine,
Muscatine, Iowa
d: 1869 Menard County, Illinois

Isaac Turner Yoakum

b: 05 Feb 1849
Illinois
m: 12 Mar 1871
Menard County,
Illinois
d: 16 Jun 1933
Tenino, Thurston
County,
Washington

Mary Dalrymple Stewart

11

b: 20 Feb 1825
Bond, Illinois
d: 21 Jun 1909
Tenino, Thurston,
Washington

Thomas Ralph Yoakum

b: 03 Jun 1879
Mount Pleasant,
Henry, Iowa
m: 1905
d: 16 Apr 1942
Centralia, Lewis,
Washington

1

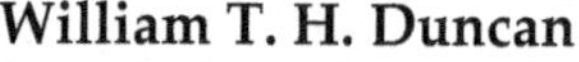

William T. H. Duncan

12

b: 10 May 1807 Cumberland
County, Kentucky
m: 08 Dec 1831 Sangamon
County, Illinois
d: 20 Oct 1862 Salisbury,
Sangamon County, Illinois

Alice Elizabeth Duncan

b: 06 Dec 1850
Sangamon County,
Illinois
d: 30 Jul 1924
Olympia, Thurston
County,
Washington

Eve Miller

13

b: 11 Dec 1813
Adair County,
Kentucky
d: 17 Apr 1895
Salisbury,
Sangamon County,
Illinois

Robert Clark MacDonald

b: 1850 Tatamagouche, Colchester, Nova Scotia, Canada
m: 16 Aug 1874 Bayhead, Colchester, Nova Scotia
d: 16 Mar 1925 Tenino, Thurston, Washington

Margaret Lyons MacDonald

b: 11 Jan 1889 Tatamagouche, Colchester, Nova Scotia, Canada
m: 07 Mar 1931 Olympia, Thurston, Washington
d: 19 May 1980 Centralia, Lewis, Washington

1

Mary Jane Stevens

b: 10 Feb 1847 Wallace, Cumberland, Nova Scotia, Canada
d: 16 Oct 1926 Centralia, Lewis, Washington

Angus MacDonald

b: 15 Apr 1822 Tatamagouche, Colchester, Nova Scotia, Canada
m:
d: 03 Jul 1906 Tatamagouche Nova Scotia, Canada

14

Ann Clark

b: 1822
d: 15 Aug 1898 Tatamagouche, Nova Scotia, Canada

Rany Stevens

b:
m:
d:

Nellie Johnson

b:
d:

Elizabeth "Ely" Hess

b: 05 Aug 1812
Westmoreland
County,
Pennsylvania
m: 1833
Pennsylvania
d: 22 Feb 1907
Macon County,
Missouri

George Henry Hess

b: 09 Jun 1780 Maryland
m: 31 Oct 1808 Herkimer or
Montgomery, NY
d: 27 Oct 1868 Ashland,
Clarion, Pennsylvania

Anna Barbara Linhart

b: 03 Feb 1785 Pennsylvania
d: 27 Jul 1866 Ashland, Clarion,
Pennsylvania

John Adam Linhart

b: 1765 York, York,
Pennsylvania
m: 1794 Pitt, Allegheny,
Pennsylvania
d: 05 Jul 1848 Wilkins,
Alleghany, Pennsylvania

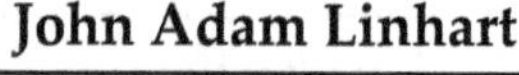 **15**

Maria Sara Baughman

b: 06 Jun 1771 Upper Hanover,
Montgomery, Pennsylvania
d: 1827 Wilkins, Alleghany,
Pennsylvania

 **16**

 **2**

William Henry Long

b: 25 Nov 1824
Franklin, Ohio
m:
d: 10 Feb 1892
Chehalis, Lewis,
Washington

2

William Long

b: 24 Jan 1781
Colchester, Nova
Scotia, Canada
m: 16 Jun 1813
Franklin, Ohio
d: 09 Jan 1851
Columbus, Ohio

**Rebekah Morrison
Suddick**

b: 10 Jul 1790 Nova Scotia,
Canada
d: 22 Jan 1864 Columbus,
Franklin, Ohio

William M Long

b: 20 Jul 1744 Medford,
Middlesex, Massachusetts
m: 1777 Colchester, Nova
Scotia, Canad
d: 08 Apr 1824 Chillicothe,
Ross, Ohio

Margaret Archibald

b: 1760 Truro, Rockingham,
New Hampshire
d: 02 May 1799 Chilicothe,
Ross, Ohio

Socelia Wirick

b: 28 Mar 1827
Lebanon,
Pennsylvania
m:
d: 12 Dec 1868
Henry County,
Iowa

Jacob Weirich Weirig

b:
m:
d:

Magdalene R

b:
d:

2

Charles Perry Anderson

b: 24 Mar 1825 Kentucky
m: 16 Mar 1851 Nodaway,
Missouri
d: 23 Sep 1905 Centralia,
Lewis, Washington

3

James Anderson

b: Abt. 1802
m:
d: 25 Jun 1852

Elizabeth Clifton

b: 02 Apr 1803 Indianna
d: 1902

John Clifton

b: Deleware
m:
d:

George Washington Yoakum Sr.

17

b: 16 Jan 1752 Peach Creek, Virginia
m: 1777 Greenbrier, West Virginia
d: 28 Oct 1800 Cumberland Mountains, Grainger County, Tennessee

James Yoakum

b: 1787 Greenbrier County, West Virginia
m: 1810 Claiborne County, Tennessee
d: 1834 Menard County, Illinois

Martha Van Bibber

18

b: 1754 Greenbrier, Virginia
d: 1829 Salisbury, Sangamon County, Illinois

Edward C. Yoakum

b: 02 Mar 1814 Claiborne County, Tennessee
m: 04 Jul 1839 Muscatine, Muscatine, Iowa
d: 1869 Menard County, Illinois

4

William Owens

b: 1750 Sussex County, Delaware
m: 28 Jan 1775 Caroline County, Maryland
d: 1815

Julia Owens

b: 1787 Claiborne, Tennessee
d: 1832 Menard County, Illinois

Elizabeth Meffin

b:
d:

Rev. William McCallen Stewart

b: 24 Apr 1794 On the Monongahela River, near Brownsville, Fayette, Pennsylvania
m: 22 Feb 1816 Adams, Ohio
d: 12 Nov 1885 Puyallup, Pierce, Washington

Rev. Robert Stewart Sr.

19

b: 28 Dec 1762 Clough, Antrim, Ireland
m:
d: 18 Mar 1846 Greenville, Bond, Illinois

Margaret McCallen

20

b: 1767 Brownsville, Pennsylvania
d: 19 May 1821 Adams, Brown, Ohio

Mary Dalrymple Stewart

b: 20 Feb 1825 Bond, Illinois
m: 04 Jul 1839 Muscatine, Muscatine, Iowa
d: 21 Jun 1909 Tenino, Thurston, Washington

4

Ann Laughlin

b: 21 May 1795 Pendleton, Anderson, South Carolina
d: 23 Mar 1847 Cedar Rapids, Linn, Iowa

John Laughlin Jr.

21

b: 16 Sep 1769 Big Spring, Cumberland, Pennsylvania
m: 16 Jun 1794 Pendleton, South Carolina
d: 27 Sep 1852 Shoal Creek, Bond, Illinois

Mary Dalrymple

22

b: 16 Jun 1776 Pendleton, Anderson, South Carolina
d: 16 Jun 1867 Union Grove, Putnam, Illinois

William T. H. Duncan

b: 10 May 1807 Cumberland
County, Kentucky
m: 08 Dec 1831 Sangamon
County, Illinois
d: 20 Oct 1862 Salisbury,
Sangamon County, Illinois

4

Marshall Duncan

b: 1783 Stokes, North Carolina
m:
d: 03 Dec 1858 Salisbury,
Sangamon, Illinois

Rachel Thrasher

b: 03 Aug 1785 Kentucky
d:

James Duncan

b: 1755 Rowan, Surry, North
Carolina
m: 1774 North Carolina
d: 1840 Salisbury, Sangamon,
Illinois

23

Averilla "Ava" Shelton

b: 1755 Surry, North Carolina
d: 1834 Salisbury, Sangamon,
Illinois

24

William Thrasher

b: 1745 England
m:
d: Mar 1796 Burke County,
North Carolina

Sarah Elizabeth Phillips

b: 24 Aug 1755 Westerleigh,
Gloucestershire, England
d: 1805 Burke, North Carolina

Eve Miller

b: 11 Dec 1813
Adair County,
Kentucky
m: 08 Dec 1831
Sangamon County,
Illinois
d: 17 Apr 1895
Salisbury,
Sangamon County,
Illinois

4

Solomon Miller

b: 11 May 1796
Adair, Kentucky
m: 13 Aug 1813
Adair County,
Kentucky
d: 07 Jun 1857
Salisbury,
Sangamon, Illinois

Nancy Ann Antle

b: 26 Dec 1792
Lincoln, Kentucky
d: 01 Apr 1854
Salisbury,
Sangamon, Illinois

George Miller

b: 1747 Darmstadt, Hesse,
Germany
m:
d: 1804 Crocus, Adair,
Kentucky

Elizabeth Beaxton

b: 1752 Port Royal, Caroline,
Virginia
d: 1832 Crocus, Adair,
Kentucky

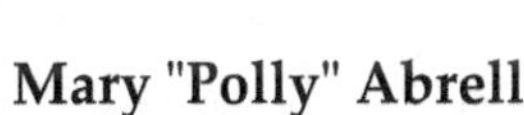

Henry Antle Sr.

b: 1753 Bullskin Run, Frederick,
Virginia
m: 1771 Winchester, Frederick,
Virginia
d: 1805 Cumberland, Kentucky

25

Mary "Polly" Abrell

b: 1752 Green, Forest,
Pennsylvania
d: 15 Aug 1823 Sangamon,
Illinois

26

Roderick MacDonald

b: Scotland
m:
d: 1842

Hugh MacDonald

b: 1795 Scotland
m:
d: 06 Oct 1860 Wallace Harbor,
Nova Scotia, Canada

? Christian

b:
d:

Angus MacDonald

b: 15 Apr 1822 Tatamagouche,
Colchester, Nova Scotia,
Canada
m:
d: 03 Jul 1906 Tatamagouche
Nova Scotia, Canada

5

Mary ?

b:
d:

John Adam Linhart

b: 1765 York, York,
Pennsylvania
m: 1794 Pitt, Allegheny,
Pennsylvania
d: 05 Jul 1848 Wilkins,
Alleghany, Pennsylvania

6

Christian Lenhart

b: 1722 Germany
m: 05 Jun 1764 York,
Pennsylvania
d: 15 Apr 1810 Wilkens Twp,
Allegheny, Pennsylvania

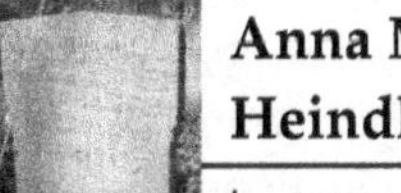 Anna Maria
Heindler

b: 1740 Germany
d: 09 Feb 1827
Wilkins, Allegheny,
Pennsylvania

 Johan Peter
Lenhart

27

b: 04 May 1708...
m: 1732...
d: 04 Apr 1774...

Maria Margaretha

b: 28 Sep 1715 Zweibrücken,
Zweibrucken, Rheinland-Pfalz,
Germany
d: 01 Jul 1777 Dover, York,
Pennsylvania

Johan Adam Heindler

b: 1720 Germany
m:
d: 1790 Pennsylvania

Heinrich Baughman Jr.

b: 1742 Hamburg, Germany
m: 1764 Montgomery, Pennsylvania
d: 18 May 1814 North Huntingdon, Westmoreland, Pennsylvania, United States

Heinrich Baughman

b: Jan 1717 Ibersheim, Worms, Rheinland-Pfalz, Germany
m: 1747
d: 30 Dec 1769 Upper Saucon, Northampton, Pennsylvania

Anne

b: 1718 Germany
d: 1758 Montgomery, Pennsylvania

Maria Sara Baughman

b: 06 Jun 1771 Upper Hanover, Montgomery, Pennsylvania
m: 1794 Pitt, Allegheny, Pennsylvania
d: 1827 Wilkins, Alleghany, Pennsylvania

Anna Catherina Kunkle

b: 25 Sep 1745 Fleorsbach, Geinhausen, Hessen, Germany
d: 10 May 1814 Irwin, Westmoreland, Pennsylvania

Johannes Kunkle

b: 21 Sep 1703 Florsbach, Gelnhausen, Hessen, Germany
m:
d: 1774 North Hampton Co., Pennsylvania

Anna Magdalena Kaiser

b: 1711 Gelnhausen, Main-Kinzig-Kreis, Hessen, Germany
d: 1798 North Hampton Co., Pennsylvania

George Washington Yoakum Sr.

b: 16 Jan 1752 Peach Creek, Virginia
m: 1777 Greenbrier, West Virginia
d: 28 Oct 1800 Cumberland Mountains, Grainger County, Tennessee

10

Valentine "Felty" Yoakum

b: 08 Sep 1722 Edigheim, Bayern, Germany
m: 1748 Hardy, West Virginia
d: 17 Jul 1763 Muddy Creek Massacre, Greenbrier, Virginia

Margaret See

b: 1725 Mohawk, Schoharie, New York
d: 11 Mar 1815 Franklin, Coshocton, Ohio

Mathias Joachim

30

b: 1699 Edigheim, Bayern, Germany
m: 18 Feb 1721 Edigheim, Bayern, Germany
d: 08 Feb 1783 Muddy Creek, Greenbrier, West Virginia

Maria Barbara Uhngefehr

b: 1698 Edigheim, Bayern, Germany
d: 1730 Died at sea

Johann George Zeh Jr.

b: 1688 Ruhlsheim, Bayern, Germany
m:
d: 23 Apr 1751 Moorefield, Hardy, West Virginia

Mary Margaret Tschudi

31

b: 1684 Frenkendorf, Basel-Country, Switzerland
d: 14 Feb 1758 Hampshire, Virginia

Peter Van Bibber Sr.

b: 25 May 1695 Cecil, Maryland
m: 1720 Maryland
d: 06 Apr 1769 Lunenburg,
Lunenburg, Virginia

32

Ann Honriette Gooding

b: 1718 Maryland
d: 1769 Virginia

Rev. Isaac Michael Van Bibber Sr.

b: 02 Feb 1724 Strasburg,
Chester, Pennsylvania
m: 1750 North Carolina
d: 10 Oct 1774 Battle of Point
Pleasant, Mason, West Virginia

Sarah Davis

b: 1725 Strasburg, Chester,
Pennsylvania
d: 05 Jan 1800 Greenbrier,
Virginia

Martha Van Bibber

b: 1754 Greenbrier, Virginia
m: 1777 Greenbrier, West
Virginia
d: 1829 Salisbury, Sangamon
County, Illinois

10

Rev. Robert Stewart Sr.

b: 28 Dec 1762
Clough, Antrim,
Ireland
m:
d: 18 Mar 1846
Greenville, Bond,
Illinois

11

Rev. William M. Stewart

b: 1722 Clough, Antrim, Ireland
m: 07 Jul 1762 Clough, Antrim,
Ireland
d: 1804 Adams, Brown, Ohio

Ann Park

b: 1725 Clough, Antrim, Ireland
d: 1787 Cumberland Valle,
Fayette, Pennsylvania

Robert Thomas Stewart

b: Abt. 1696 Clough, Antrim,
Ireland
m:
d: Clough, Antrim, Ireland

Rachel Maxwell

b: Sep 1700 Scotland
d: Ireland

Robert McCallen

b: 01 May 1749
Pennsylvania
m:
d: 25 Dec 1821
Harrison, Harrison,
Indiana

Margaret McCallen

b: 1767 Brownsville,
Pennsylvania
m:
d: 19 May 1821 Adams, Brown,
Ohio

11

Daniel Bradley

b: 20 May 1729 Fairfield,
Connecticut
m:
d: 13 Dec 1780 Fairfield,
Connecticut

33

Mary Bradley

b: 14 Oct 1752
Connecticut
d: 12 Oct 1821
Palmyra,
Washington,
Indiana

Margaret

b:
d:

John Laughlin Jr.

b: 16 Sep 1769 Big Spring,
Cumberland, Pennsylvania
m: 16 Jun 1794 Pendleton,
South Carolina
d: 27 Sep 1852 Shoal Creek,
Bond, Illinois

11

John Luke Laughlin Sr.

b: 1734 Antrim, Northern
Ireland
m: 1759 Philadelphia,
Pennsylvania
d: 1774 Pendleton District,
South Carolina

Mary White

b: 1745 Quenbey, Scotland
d: 1773 Caldwell County,
Kentucky

William Laughlin

b: 1700 Antrim, Antrim, Ireland
m:
d: Pendleton, Anderson, South
Carolina

Nancy Hodges

b: 1710 Ireland
d: Pennsylvania

Anthony White

b: Abt. 1700 Luenberg,
Scotland
m:
d:

Mary Ralston

b: Luenberg, Scotland
d:

George Dalrymple  **34**

b: 1709 Dalmahoy, Midlothian, Scotland
m: 23 Aug 1731 Philadelphia, Pennsylvania
d: 1764 Laurens, South Carolina

Samuel Dalrymple

b: 1755 Newberry, Newberry, South Carolina
m: 1771 Laurens, Laurens, South Carolina
d: 1791 Abbeville, Abbeville, South Carolina

Rose Mason **35**

b: 1705 Philadelphia, Pennsylvania
d: Unknown Laurens, South Carolina

Mary Dalrymple

b: 16 Jun 1776 Pendleton, Anderson, South Carolina
m: 16 Jun 1794 Pendleton, South Carolina
d: 16 Jun 1867 Union Grove, Putnam, Illinois

11

James Pollock

b: 1720 Pennsylvania, Somerset, Pennsylvania
m:
d: 1793 Anderson, South Carolina

Sarah Pollock

b: 1755 Pendleton, Anderson, South Carolina
d: Feb 1837 Pendleton, Anderson, South Carolina

Ann Wilson

b: 1724 Pennsylvania, Somerset, Pennsylvania
d: Newberry, South Carolina

Marshall Duncan

b: 1700 Dunfries, Prince
William, Virginia
m: 1730 Prince William,
Virginia
d: May 1777 Snow Creek, Surry,
North Carolina

William Duncan

b: 01 Oct 1659 Perth,
Perthshire, Scotland
m:
d: 1720 Northern Neck,
Culpeper, Virginia

36

Margaret McMurde

b: 1661 Dumfries-shire,
Scotland
d: 1720 Bellhaven, Alexandria,
Virginia, USA

James Duncan

b: 1755 Rowan, Surry, North
Carolina
m: 1774 North Carolina
d: 1840 Salisbury, Sangamon,
Illinois

12

Mary Ann Durron

b: 1705 Prince William, Virginia
d: May 1777 Snow Creek, Surry,
North Carolina

John Shelton

b: 19 Jul 1722 Middlesex,
Virginia
m:
d: 1803 Rockingham county,
North Carolina

Averilla "Ava" Shelton

b: 1755 Surry, North Carolina
m: 1774 North Carolina
d: 1834 Salisbury, Sangamon,
Illinois

12

Elizabeth Lawson

b: 1740 Virginia
d: 1801 Madison County,
Kentucky

David Lawson

b: 1730 Bedford, Virginia
m:
d: 1830 Stokes, North Carolina

37

Frances

b: 1718 Virginia
d:

Henry Antil

b: 1691 Minchinhampton,
Horsley, Gloucestershire,
England
m:
d: 1760 Frederick, Virginia

38

Margery Smith

b: 1695 England
d: 1718 Virginia

Peter Antle

b: 1718 Minchinhampton,
Gloucestershire, England
m:
d: 06 Mar 1771 Winchester,
Frederick, Virginia

Henry Antle Sr.

b: 1753 Bullskin Run, Frederick,
Virginia
m: 1771 Winchester, Frederick,
Virginia
d: 1805 Cumberland, Kentucky

13

Ann ??

b: 1727 England?
d: 1787 Winchester, Frederick,
Virginia

Mary "Polly" Abrell

b: 1752 Green, Forest,
Pennsylvania
m: 1771 Winchester, Frederick,
Virginia
d: 15 Aug 1823 Sangamon,
Illinois

13

John Abrell

b: 17 Dec 1720 Zürich, Zurich,
Switzerland
m:
d: 06 Jun 1772 Berkeley, South
Carolina

Anna Maria Lang

b: 31 Jul 1729 Stadel, Zurich,
Switzerland
d: Orangeburng, South
Carolina

Hans Jacob Lang

b: 28 Nov 1686 Ober Raat,
Stadel Parish, Zurich,
Switzerland
m: 05 Dec 1717 Stadel, Zurich,
Switzerland
d: 24 Jan 1740 Raat, Zurich,
Switzerland

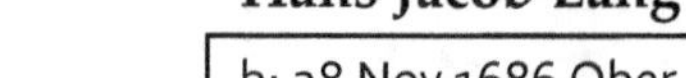

39

Anna Meyer

b: 13 May 1697 Raat, Zurich,
Switzerland
d: 24 Jan 1740 Switzerland

40

Johan Peter Lenhart

b: 04 May 1708 Horn, Rhein-Hunsruck-Kreis, Rheinland-Pfalz, Germany
m: 1732 Rheinland-Pfalz, Germany
d: 04 Apr 1774 Dover, York, Pennsylvania

15

Johann Christopfell Lenhart

b: 1670 Benzweiler, Rhein-Hunsruck-Kreis, Rheinland-Pfalz, Germany
m:
d: 16 Mar 1756 Klosterkumbd, Rhein-Hunsruck-Kreis, Rheinland-Pfalz, Germany

Anna Eva Kessler

b: 21 Mar 1674 Rheinland-Pfalz, Germany
d: 30 Jan 1743 Horn, Lower Austria, Austria

Hans Velten Leonhardt

41

b: Unknown...
m: 1674
d: 23 Jan 1716...

Anna Catherina Schell

b: 1648 Mörschbach, Rhein-Hunsruck-Kreis, Rheinland-Pfalz, Germany
d: 13 Jan 1733 Benzweiler, Rhein-Hunsruck-Kreis, Rheinland-Pfalz, Germany

Hans Peter Kessler

42

b: 1640 Klosterkumbd, Rhein-Hunsruck-Kreis, Rheinland-Pfalz, Germany
m: 13 Oct 1663 Horn, Rhein-Hunsruck-Kreis, Rheinland-Pfalz, Germany
d: 12 May 1694 Klosterkumbd, Rhein-Hunsruck-Kreis, Rheinland-Pfalz, Germany

Anna Christina Peters

b: 1640 Klosterkumbd, Rhein-Hunsruck-Kreis, Rheinland-Pfalz, Germany
d: 26 May 1694 Klosterkumbd, Rhein-Hunsruck-Kreis, Rheinland-Pfalz, Germany

Heinrich Baughman

b: Jan 1717 Ibersheim, Worms, Rheinland-Pfalz, Germany

m: 1747

d: 30 Dec 1769 Upper Saucon, Northampton, Pennsylvania

16

Johann George Bachmann

b: 02 May 1686 Richterswil, Canton, Zurich, Switzerland

m: 1715 Ibersheim, Worms, Rheinhessen-Pfalz, Rheinland-Pfalz, Germany

d: 19 Nov 1753 Upper Saucon, Lehigh, Pennsylvania

Anna Maria Schnebelli

b: 12 Apr 1698 Ibersheim, Worms, Rheinland-Pfalz, Germany

d: 04 Nov 1776 Upper Saucon, Lehigh, Pennsylvania

Jodocus Bachman

43

b: 03 Aug 1657 Richterswil, Zurich Canton, Switzerland

m: 12 Feb 1677 Richterswil,Zurich Canton,,Switzerland

d: 19 Aug 1736 Richterswil, Zurich Canton, Switzerland

Regula Treichler

44

b: 1646 Richterswil, Zurich Canton, Switzerland

d: 26 Jan 1706 Richterswil, Zurich Canton, Switzerland

Johannes Jacob Schnebelli

b:

m:

d:

Elisabeth

b:

d:

Johann Sebastian Kunkle

b: 18 Feb 1675 Gelnhausen, Main-Kinzig-Kreis, Hessen, Germany
m:
d: 14 Oct 1737 Gelnhausen, Main-Kinzig-Kreis, Hessen, Germany

Johannes Kunkle

b: 21 Sep 1703 Florsbach, Gelnhausen, Hessen, Germany
m:
d: 1774 North Hampton Co., Pennsylvania

16

Anna Catharina Samer

b: 10 Dec 1677 Gelnhausen, Main-Kinzig-Kreis, Hessen, Germany
d: 04 Mar 1744 Gelnhausen, Main-Kinzig-Kreis, Hessen, Germany

Phillip Jochem

b: Mors, Germany
m:
d:

Mathias Joachim

b: 1699 Edigheim, Bayern, Germany
m: 1727
d: 08 Feb 1783 Muddy Creek, Greenbrier, West Virginia

17

Martin Von Tschudi → 45

b: 27 Apr 1591 Basel, Basel Town, Switzerland
m: 03 Oct 1614 Hunzah, Basel, Switzerland
d: 1637 Frankendorf, Basel, Switzerland

Jakob Von Tschudi

b: 09 Aug 1635 Frenkendorf, Basel-Landschaft, Switzerland
m: 30 May 1671 Frenkendorf, Basel-Country, Switzerland
d: 1727 Frenkendorf, Basel-Landschaft, Switzerland

Margred Grufin Brevin

b: Mar 1591 Lausen, Basel, Switzerland
d: 18 Mar 1665 Frankendorf, Canton Basel, Switzerland

Mary Margaret Tschudi

b: 1684 Frenkendorf, Basel-Country, Switzerland
m:
d: 14 Feb 1758 Hampshire, Virginia

← 17

Niclaus Schaub → 46

b:
m: 27 Feb 1638 Basel, Basel Town, Switzerland
d:

Elsbeth Schwab

b: 08 Jan 1636 Frenkendorf, Basel-Landschaft, Switzerland
d: Unknown Frenkendorf, Basel-Landschaft, Switzerland

Barbara Marti → 47

b:
d:

Jacob Isaac Van Bibber

48

b: Abt. 1643 Duchy of Cleves, Utretch, Netherlands
m: 1660 Krefeld, Krefeld, Nordrhein-Westfalen, Germany
d: 07 Sep 1705 Germantown, Pennsylvania

Christina Hermania

b: 1643 Duchy of Cleves, Utretch, Netherlands
d: 05 Sep 1711 Philadelphia, Pennsylvania

Isaac Jacob Van Bibber

b: 1661 Duchy of Cleves, Utretch, Netherlands
m: 25 May 1690 Pennsylvania
d: 14 Sep 1723 Cecil County, Maryland

Peter Van Bibber Sr.

b: 25 May 1695 Cecil, Maryland
m: 1720 Maryland
d: 06 Apr 1769 Lunenburg, Lunenburg, Virginia

18

Frances Schumaker

b: 1669 St. Stephen's Parish
d:

Daniel Bradley

b: 20 May 1729 Fairfield,
Connecticut
m:
d: 13 Dec 1780 Fairfield,
Connecticut

20

Daniel Bradley

b: 11 Jun 1704 Fairfield,
Connecticut
m: 11 Jun 1724 Fairfield,
Connecticut
d: 23 Apr 1765 Ridgefield,
Fairfield, Connecticut

Esther Burr

b: 31 Jan 1703 Fairfield,
Connecticut
d: 29 Dec 1741 Ridgefield,
Fairfield, Connecticut

Daniel Bradley

b: 1673 Fairfield, Connecticut
m: 1697
d: 01 Jul 1713 Fairfield,
Connecticut

49

Abigail Jackson

b: 1676 Fairfield, Connecticut
d: 1714 Fairfield, Connecticut

50

Daniel Burr

b: 1660 Fairfield, Connecticut
m:
d: 01 Aug 1727 Fairfield,
Connecticut

51

Elizabeth Pinckney

b: 1675 Fairfield, Connecticut
d: 1722 Fairfield, Connecticut

52

George Dalrymple

b: 1709 Dalmahoy, Midlothian, Scotland
m: 23 Aug 1731 Philadelphia, Pennsylvania
d: 1764 Laurens, South Carolina

22

John Dalrymple 1st Earl of Stair

b: 1648 Stair, Kyle, Ayrshire, Scotland
m: 19 Jan 1669 Scotland
d: 08 Jan 1707 Edinburgh, Midlothian, Scotland

Elizabeth Dundas

b: 1650 Newliston, West Lothian, Scotland
d: 25 May 1731 Edinburgh, Midlothian, Scotland

Sir James Dalrymple 1st Viscount of Stair

b: May 1619 Barr,...
m: 21 Sep 1643...
d: 29 Nov 1695 St...

53

Margaret Ross

b: 1623 Balneil, Wigtownshire, Scotland
d: 1692 Edinburgh, Midlothian, Scotland

54

Sir John Dundas 9th of Newliston Craigton and Duddingston

b: 1615 Kirkliston, West Lothian, Scotland
m:
d: 1655

55

Agnes Gray

b: 05 Dec 1622 Edinburgh, Midlothian, Scotland
d: 1699 Edinburgh, Midlothian, Scotland

56

John Mason

b: 1735 Berkeley, South Carolina

m:

d: 15 Nov 1783 Indian Creek, Berkeley, South Carolina

Rose Mason

b: 1705 Philadelphia, Pennsylvania

m: 23 Aug 1731 Philadelphia, Pennsylvania

d: Unknown Laurens, South Carolina

22

Eleanor Lewis

b: 1740 Berkeley, South Carolina

d: 1783 South Carolina

John Duncan

57

b: 1612 St Ninians,
Stirlingshire, Scotland
m:
d: 1630 Dundee, Angus,
Scotland

Janet Macarthur

b: 1600 Scotland
d: Scotland

Rev. William Duncan

b: 07 Jan 1630 Perth,
Perthshire, Scotland
m: 29 Aug 1657 Glasgow,
Lanarkshire, Scotland
d: 02 Jan 1692 Glasgow,
Lanarkshire, Scotland

William Duncan

b: 01 Oct 1659 Perth,
Perthshire, Scotland
m:
d: 1720 Northern Neck,
Culpeper, Virginia

23

David Lawson

b: 1730 Bedford, Virginia

m:

d: 1830 Stokes, North Carolina

24

David Lawson

b: 1710 Bedford, Virginia

m:

d: 1803 Virginia

Henry Antil

b: 1691 Minchinhampton,
Horsley, Gloucestershire,
England
m:
d: 1760 Frederick, Virginia

25

James Antill

b: 30 Mar 1660 Horsley,
Gloucestershire, England
m: 30 Mar 1689
d: 1755 Virginia

Frances Burford

b: 1660 Marlyand
d:

Richard Antille

b: 1630 London, London,
England
m:
d: Horsley, Gloucestershire,
England

Thomas Justice Burford

b: 1630 England
m:
d: 24 Mar 1686 Charles,
Maryland, United States

Ann Pope

b: 1639 St. Mary's County,
Maryland
d: May 1700 Charles, Maryland,
United States

Jakob Lang

b: 04 Mar 1660 Stadel, Zurich,
Switzerland
m: 01 Nov 1681 Stadel Parish,
Zurich, Switzerland
d: 19 Jul 1720 Raat, Zurich,
Switzerland

Junghans Lang

b: 11 Feb 1627 Stadel, Zurich,
Switzerland
m: 20 Nov 1645 Stadel, Zurich,
Switzerland
d: 26 Jun 1692 Raat, Zurich,
Switzerland

58

Elsbeth Surber

b: 07 Jan 1627 Niederhori,
Bulach, Switzerland
d: 14 Jun 1715 Raat,
Switzerland

59

Hans Jacob Lang

b: 28 Nov 1686 Ober Raat,
Stadel Parish, Zurich,
Switzerland
m: 05 Dec 1717 Stadel, Zurich,
Switzerland
d: 24 Jan 1740 Raat, Zurich,
Switzerland

26

Elsbeth Muller

b: 30 Aug 1657 Nassenbail,
Niedechasli, Switzerland
d: 14 Jun 1715 Raat, Zurich,
Switzerland

Jugli Meyer

b: 1671 Raat, Zurich,
Switzerland
m:
d:

Anna Meyer

b: 13 May 1697 Raat, Zurich,
Switzerland
m: 05 Dec 1717 Stadel, Zurich,
Switzerland
d: 24 Jan 1740 Switzerland

26

Elsbeth Huber

b: 1675 Raat, Zurich,
Switzerland
d: 29 Jan 1731 Riffersevel,
Switzerland

Hanss Leonhardt

b: 1587 Bischweiler, Elsass, Germany
m:
d:

Brigida Jacob

b: 1601 Bischweiler, Bas-Rhin, Alsace, France
d:

Johann Conrad Leonardt

b: 1624 Bilsdorf, Saarlouis, Saarland, Germany
m:
d: 1695 Nalbach, Saarlouis, Saarland, Germany

Hans Velten Leonhardt

b: Unknown Zweibrücken, Zweibrucken, Rheinland-Pfalz, Germany
m: 1674
d: 23 Jan 1716 Benzweiler, Rhein-Hunsruck-Kreis, Rheinland-Pfalz, Germany

Arlene Lenhart

b: 1635 Bilsdorf, Saarlouis, Saarland, Germany
d: 1705 Bilsdorf, Saarlouis, Saarland, Germany

27

Hans Peter Kessler

b: 1640 Klosterkumbd, Rhein-
Hunsruck-Kreis, Rheinland-
Pfalz, Germany
m: 13 Oct 1663 Horn, Rhein-
Hunsruck-Kreis, Rheinland-
Pfalz, Germany
d: 12 May 1694 Klosterkumbd,
Rhein-Hunsruck-Kreis,
Rheinland-Pfalz, Germany

Johannes Kessler

b: 1628 Tiefenbach, Biberach,
Baden-Wuerttemberg,
Germany
m:
d: 06 Feb 1694 Hart,
Memmingen, Bayern,
Germany

Katharina Hipp

b: 1628 Hungary
d: 16 Sep 1703 Hart,
Memmingen, Bayern,
Germany

27

Ulrich Bachman

b: 1600 Langnau, Canton,
Bern, Switzerland
m: 1630
d: 1661 Laubersweiler, Canton,
Bern, Switzerland

Anna Grog

b: 1605 Lauperswil, Canton,
Bern, Switzerland
d: 1665 Zürich, Zurich,
Switzerland

Hans Jacob Bachman

b: 1629 Richterswirl, Zurich,
Switzerland
m: 04 Oct 1653 Richterswil,
Zurich, Switzerland
d: 1704 Richterswirl, Zurich,
Switzerland

Jodocus Bachman

b: 03 Aug 1657 Richterswil,
Zurich Canton, Switzerland
m: 12 Feb 1677
Richterswil,Zurich
Canton,,Switzerland
d: 19 Aug 1736 Richterswil,
Zurich Canton, Switzerland

28

Regula Strickler

b: 1629 Richterswil, Canton,
Zurich, Switzerland
d: 20 Dec 1679 Richterswil,
Zurich, Switzerland

Regula Treichler

b: 1646 Richterswil, Zurich
Canton, Switzerland
m: 12 Feb 1677
Richterswil,Zurich
Canton,,Switzerland
d: 26 Jan 1706 Richterswil,
Zurich Canton, Switzerland

28

Heinrich Treichler

b: 1603 Richterswil, Zurich,
Switzerland
m:
d: 07 Mar 1679 Richterswil,
Zurich, Switzerland

Dorothea Hiestand

b: 1607 Richterswil, Zurich,
Switzerland
d: 13 Jul 1678 Richterswil,
Zurich, Switzerland

Martin Von Tschudi

b: 1537 Frenkendorf, Liestal,
Basel-Landschaft, Switzerland
m: 1560 Frenkendorf, Basel-
Country, Switzerland
d: Frenkendorf, Liestal, Basel-
Landschaft, Switzerland

60

Anna Salatine

b: 1541 Frenkendorf, Basel-
Country, Switzerland
d: Basel, Basel-Town,
Switzerland

Hans Von Tschudi

b: 01 Aug 1563 Frenkendorf,
Canton Basel, Switzerland
m:
d: 1594 Frenkendorf, Canton
Basel, Switzerland

Elsbeth Gyger

b: Abt. 1568 Giebenach,
Canton Basel, Switzerland
d: 1594 Frankendorf, Canton
Basel, Switzerland

Martin Von Tschudi

b: 27 Apr 1591 Basel, Basel
Town, Switzerland
m: 03 Oct 1614 Hunzah, Basel,
Switzerland
d: 1637 Frankendorf, Basel,
Switzerland

31

Hans Schaub

b: Abt. 1575 Basel, Basel Town, Switzerland
m:
d: 1610 Ziefen, Basel Town, Switzerland

Adelheit Meyer

b: Abt. 1575 Basel, Basel Town, Switzerland
d:

Niclaus Schaub

b:
m: 27 Feb 1638 Basel, Basel Town, Switzerland
d:

31

Laurentz Marti

b: Abt. 1575
m:
d:

Barbara Marti

b:
m: 27 Feb 1638 Basel, Basel
Town, Switzerland
d:

31

Willem VanVredenburg

b: 1580 Rotterdam,
Rotterdam, Zuid-Holland,
Netherlands
m:
d: 1658 Holland, Reusel-de
Mierden, Noord-Brabant,
Netherlands

Isaac Jacobs VanBebber

b: Dec 1610 Krefeld, Rhenish,
Preussen, Germany
m: 1629 Germany
d: 1690 Germantown,
Pennsylvania

Dorothea Farrill

b: 1585 Netherlands
d:

Jacob Isaac Van Bibber

b: Abt. 1643 Duchy of Cleves,
Utretch, Netherlands
m: 1660 Krefeld, Krefeld,
Nordrhein-Westfalen,
Germany
d: 07 Sep 1705 Germantown,
Pennsylvania

32

Bishop Herman Isacks Op Den Graeff

b: 26 Nov 1585 Aldekerk,
Kleve, Nordrhein-Westfalen,
Germany
m: 16 Aug 1605 Kempen,
Heinsberg, Nordrhein-
Westfalen, Germany
d: 27 Dec 1642 Krefeld,
Krefeld, Nordrhein-Westfalen,
Germany

61

Hester Op Den Graeff

b: 18 Jan 1609 Krefeld, Krefeld,
Nordrhein-Westfalen,
Germany
d: 21 Feb 1642 Germantown,
Philadelphia, Pennsylvania

Grietjen Pletjes

b: 26 Nov 1588 Kempen,
Holland
d: 17 Jan 1642/43 Krefeld,
Krefeld, Nordrhein-Westfalen,
Germany

62

Daniel Bradley

b: 1673 Fairfield, Connecticut
m: 1697
d: 01 Jul 1713 Fairfield,
Connecticut

33

Francis Bradley Sr.

b: 1625 Fairfield, Connecticut
m:
d: 22 Oct 1698 Fairfield,
Connecticut

Ruth Barlow

b: 1638 Fairfield, Connecticut
d: 22 Oct 1689 Fairfield,
Connecticut

Thomas Bradley

b: 1594 Pomfret, Yorkshire,
England
m:
d: 1636 England

Francis Savile

b: 1604 Pomfret, Yorkshire,
England
d: 30 Jan 1663 Yorkshire,
England

John Barlow

b: 1600 Manchester,
Lancashire, England
m:
d: 28 Mar 1674 Fairfield,
Connecticut

Ann Ward

b: 1604 Suffolk, England
d: 25 Feb 1684 Fairfield,
Connecticut

Joseph Jackson

b: 1649 Fairfield, Connecticut
m:
d: 31 Oct 1681 Fairfield,
Connecticut

Abigail Jackson

b: 1676 Fairfield, Connecticut
m: 1697
d: 1714 Fairfield, Connecticut

33

Mary Godwin

b: 1653 Fairfield, Connecticut
d: 28 Jul 1678 Cohansey,
Cumberland, New Jersey

Daniel Burr

b: 1660 Fairfield, Connecticut
m:
d: 01 Aug 1727 Fairfield,
Connecticut

33

Jehu Burr Jr.

b: 1625 Lavenham, Suffolk,
England
m: 20 Oct 1658 Fairfield,
Connecticut
d: 31 Oct 1692 Fairfield,
Connecticut

Esther Ward

b: 1623 Watertown, Middlesex,
Massachusetts
d: 1664 Fairfield, Connecticut

Jehu Burr Sr.

b: 1596 Essex, England
m: 1624 En
d: 1671 Fairfield, Connecticut

Elizabeth Cable

b: 1598 Essex, England
d: 1670 Fairfield, Connecticut

Andrew Ward

b: 1597 Homersfield, Suffolk,
England
m: 1627 England
d: 28 Feb 1660 Fairfield,
Connecticut

Hester Sherman

b: 01 Apr 1606 Dedham, Essex,
England
d: 28 Feb 1666 Fairfield,
Connecticut

Rev. Philip Pinckney

b: Jan 1584 Rushall Manor,
Rushall, Wiltshire, England
m: 1610 Dinton, Wiltshire,
England
d: Feb 1658 Dinton, Wiltshire,
England

63

Phillip Pinckney

b: 07 Mar 1618 Dinton,
Wiltshire, England
m: 20 Jun 1648 Fairfield,
Connecticut
d: 28 Feb 1687 Eastchester,
Westchester, New York

Margaret Gough

b: 1591 Dinton, Wiltshire,
England
d: 1618 Dinton,
Buckinghamshire, England

Elizabeth Pinckney

b: 1675 Fairfield, Connecticut
m:
d: 1722 Fairfield, Connecticut

33

George Phippen

b: 1584 Melcomb, Dorset,
England
m: 20 Jun 1648 Weymouth,
Dorset, England
d: Feb 1650 London, England

64

Jane Phippen

b: Jan 1629 England
d: Feb 1680 Eastchester,
Westchester, New York

Joan Rie Penrose

b: Jan 1589 Weymouth,
Dorset, England
d: Feb 1650 England

65

James Dalrymple

b: 1543
m:
d: 05 Aug 1586

66

Isabel Kennedy

b: 1573 Baltersane, Ayrshire, Scotland
d:

67

James Dalrymple

b: 1589 Drummurchie, Barr, Ayrshire, Scotland
m:
d: Jan 1625 Barr, Ayrshire, Scotland

Fergus Kennedy

b: 1560 Scotland
m:
d: 1635 Knockdaw, Ayrshire, Scotland

68

Sir James Dalrymple 1st Viscount of Stair

b: May 1619 Barr, Ayrshire, Scotland
m: 21 Sep 1643 Scotland
d: 29 Nov 1695 St Giles Cathedral, Edinburgh, Midlothian, Scotland

Janet Kennedy

b: 1598 Knockdaw, Scotland
d: 1663 Scotland

34

69

Robert Ross

b: 1563 Renfrewshire, Scotland
m: 1591 Scotland
d: Oct 1595 Renfrewshire, Scotland

James Ross

b: 1589 Hawkhead, Renfrewshire, Scotland
m: 1613 Scotland
d: 17 Dec 1633 Balneil, Wigtownshire, Scotland

Jean Hamilton

b: 1571 Ardross, Fife, Scotland
d: May 1631 Ardross, Fife, Scotland

Margaret Ross

b: 1623 Balneil, Wigtownshire, Scotland
m: 20 Jan 1639
d: 1692 Edinburgh, Midlothian, Scotland

34

Sarah Syme

b: 1595
d: 1623 Edinburgh, Midlothian, Scotland

Walter Dundas

b: 1580 Linlithgow, West
Lothian, Scotland
m:
d: 1622 Fermanagh, Ireland

Elizabeth Bruce

b: Linlithgow, West Lothian,
Scotland
d:

James Dundas

b: 1600 Magdalens, Scotland
m:
d: 1637 Fermanagh, Ireland

Lady Elizabeth Douglas

b:
d:

**Sir John Dundas 9th of
Newliston Craigton and
Duddingston**

b: 1615 Kirkliston, West
Lothian, Scotland
m:
d: 1655

34

Thomas Gray

b: 1559 Barony, Lanarkshire,
Scotland
m:
d: 1671 Kirkoswald, Ayrshire,
Scotland

Margaret Walker

b: 1563 Barony, Lanarkshire,
Scotland
d:

William Gray

b: 1600 Pittendrum, Scotland
m: 20 Jun 1620 Midlothian,
Scotland
d: 04 Aug 1648 Edinburgh,
Midlothian, Scotland

Egidia Smith

b: 1603 Grothill, Midlothian,
Scotland
d: 17 Sep 1686 Midlothian,
Scotland

Agnes Gray

b: 05 Dec 1622 Edinburgh,
Midlothian, Scotland
m: 1663 Edinburgh,
Midlothian, Scotland
d: 1699 Edinburgh, Midlothian,
Scotland

34

70

John Duncan

b: 1530 Edinburgh, Midlothian, Scotland
m:
d: 1620 Perth, Perthshire, Scotland

Jenet Andro

b: 1535 Edinburgh, Midlothian, Scotland
d: 1635 Glasgow, Lanarkshire, Scotland

Andrew Duncan

b: 1575 Perth, Perthshire, Scotland
m:
d: 1605 Dauiot, Aberdeenshire, Scotland

John Duncan

b: 1612 St Ninians, Stirlingshire, Scotland
m:
d: 1630 Dundee, Angus, Scotland

Chippewa Indian

b: 1580 United States
d: 1625 Scotland

36

Junghans Lang

b: 11 Feb 1627 Stadel, Zurich,
Switzerland
m: 20 Nov 1645 Stadel, Zurich,
Switzerland
d: 26 Jun 1692 Raat, Zurich,
Switzerland

39

Hans Lang

b: 06 Feb 1588 Windlach,
Zurich, Switzerland
m: 28 Jun 1612 Stadel Parish,
Zurich, Switzerland
d: 12 Jul 1663 Windlach,
Zurich, Switzerland

Margreth Volkhart

b: 1591 Nschikon, Niedechasli,
Switzerland
d: 26 Jan 1651 Windlach,
Zurich, Switzerland

Hans Lang

b: 1554 Windlach, Zurich,
Switzerland
m:
d: 1591 Windlach, Zurich,
Switzerland

Elsbeth Baumgartner

b: 1556 Windlach, Zurich,
Switzerland
d: 1591

Heinrich Surber

b: 1571 Bülach, Zurich,
Switzerland
m:
d:

Anna Koch

b: 1575 Zürich, Zurich,
Switzerland
d:

Hans Surber

b: 1600 Switzerland
m:
d: 21 Aug 1664

Elsbeth Kempf

b: 1602
d:

Elsbeth Surber

b: 07 Jan 1627 Niederhori,
Bulach, Switzerland
m: 20 Nov 1645 Stadel, Zurich,
Switzerland
d: 14 Jun 1715 Raat,
Switzerland

39

Martin Von Tschudi

b: 1537 Frenkendorf, Liestal,
Basel-Landschaft, Switzerland
m: 1560 Frenkendorf, Basel-
Country, Switzerland
d: Frenkendorf, Liestal, Basel-
Landschaft, Switzerland

45

Hans Von Tschudi

b: 1513 Frenkendorf, Basel-
Country, Switzerland
m: 1535 Basel, Basel Town,
Switzerland
d: 1538 Frenkendorf, Basel-
Country, Switzerland

Elsa Barth

b: 1520 Lausen, Basel,
Switzerland
d: Basel, Basel Town,
Switzerland

William I Duke of Cleves

b: 18 Jul 1516...
m:
d: 05 Jan 1592...

71

John William De La Marck

b: 28 May 1562
m:
d: 25 Mar 1609

Maria Habsburg of Austria

b: 15 May 1531 Wien, Vienna, Austria
d: 11 Dec 1581 Hambach, Duren, Nordrhein-Westfalen, Germany

72

Bishop Herman Isacks Op Den Graeff

b: 26 Nov 1585 Aldekerk, Kleve, Nordrhein-Westfalen, Germany
m: 16 Aug 1605 Kempen, Heinsberg, Nordrhein-Westfalen, Germany
d: 27 Dec 1642 Krefeld, Krefeld, Nordrhein-Westfalen, Germany

Anna Van Aldekerk

b:
d:

48

Grietjen Pletjes

b: 26 Nov 1588 Kempen,
Holland
m: 16 Aug 1605 Kempen,
Heinsberg, Nordrhein-
Westfalen, Germany
d: 17 Jan 1642/43 Krefeld,
Krefeld, Nordrhein-Westfalen,
Germany

48

Driessen Andreas Pletjes

b: 1555 Kempen, Rheinland,
Prussia
m: 13 Dec 1584 Kempen,
Rheinland, Prussia
d: 22 May 1608 Kempen,
Rheinland, Prussia

Alet Gobels Syllys

b: 1563 Kempen, Rheinland,
Prussia
d: 1615 Krefeld, Krefeld,
Nordrhein-Westfalen,
Germany

Rev. Philip Pinckney

b: Jan 1584 Rushall Manor,
Rushall, Wiltshire, England
m: 1610 Dinton, Wiltshire,
England
d: Feb 1658 Dinton, Wiltshire,
England

52

William Pynkne

b: 1541 England
m:
d: 1594 Rushall, Staffordshire,
England

Anna Webb

b: 1553 Lidgate, Suffolk,
England
d: England

George Phippen

b: 1584 Melcomb, Dorset,
England
m: 20 Jun 1648 Weymouth,
Dorset, England
d: Feb 1650 London, England

52

Robert Phippen

b: 1555 Weymouth, Dorset,
England
m:
d: 12 Oct 1589 Melcombe
Regis, Dorset, England

Cecily Jordan

b: 1559 Weymouth, Dorset,
England
d: 1603 Weymouth, Dorset,
England

Joan Rie Penrose

b: Jan 1589 Weymouth,
Dorset, England
m: 20 Jun 1648 Weymouth,
Dorset, England
d: Feb 1650 England

52

John Penros

b: 1579 Manaccan, Cornwall,
England
m:
d: England

Jane Trefusis

b: 1588 Cornwall, England
d: 1660

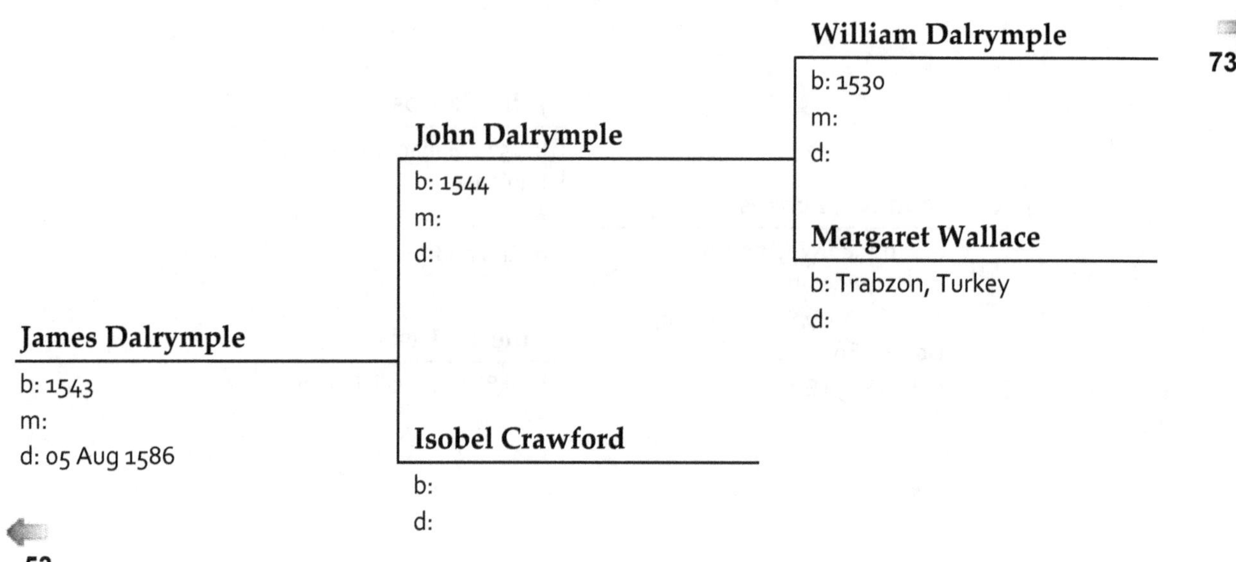

William Dalrymple
b: 1530
m:
d:
73
John Dalrymple
b: 1544
m:
d:
Margaret Wallace
b: Trabzon, Turkey
d:
James Dalrymple
b: 1543
m:
d: 05 Aug 1586
Isobel Crawford
b:
d:
53

Isabel Kennedy

b: 1573 Baltersane, Ayrshire,
Scotland
m:
d:

53

Thomas Kennedy

b: 1534 Bargany, Ayrshire,
Scotland
m:
d: 1597

Agnes Montgomerie

b: 1541 Cunninghame,
Ayrshire, Scotland
d: Bargany, Ayrshire, Scotland

David Kennedy Kennedy

b: 1520 Maybole, Ayrshire, Scotland
m:
d: 1582 Knockdaw, Ayrshire, Scotland

Fergus Kennedy

b: 1560 Scotland
m:
d: 1635 Knockdaw, Ayrshire, Scotland

53

James Ross

b: 1517 Renfrewshire, Scotland
m:
d: 02 Apr 1581 Renfrewshire,
Scotland

Jean Sempill

b: 1543 Renfrew, Renfrewshire,
Scotland
d: 28 Feb 1592 Hawkhead,
Renfrewshire, Scotland

Robert Ross

b: 1563 Renfrewshire, Scotland
m: 1591 Scotland
d: Oct 1595 Renfrewshire,
Scotland

54

Allan Duncan

b: 1460 Garbred, Fife, Scotland
m:
d: 27 May 1574 Scotland

William Duncan

b: 1501 Dunfermline, Fife,
Scotland
m:
d: 27 May 1574 Paisley,
Renfrewshire, Scotland

Jonat Crosby

b: 1460 Garbred, Scotland
d: Scotland

John Duncan

b: 1530 Edinburgh, Midlothian,
Scotland
m:
d: 1620 Perth, Perthshire,
Scotland

57

George Robinson

b: 1460 Govan, Lanarkshire,
Scotland
m:
d: 1550 Govan, Lanarkshire,
Scotland

Agnes Robinson

b: 1509 Dunfermline, Fife,
Scotland
d: 1597 Scotland

John II Duke of Cleves

b: 1458 Bruxelles, Brabant, Belgium

m: 1490

d: 1521 Cleve, Gutersloh, Nordrhein-Westfalen, Germany

74

Mathilde of Hesse

b: 04 Jul 1473 Blankenstein, Ennepe-Ruhr-Kreis, Nordrhein-Westfalen, Germany

d: 19 Feb 1505 Oder, Brandenburg, Germany

John III Duke of Cleves

b: 10 Nov 1490

m:

d: 06 Feb 1538

William I Duke of Cleves

b: 18 Jul 1516 Dusseldorf, Nordrhein-Westfalen, Germany

m:

d: 05 Jan 1592 Dusseldorf, Nordrhein-Westfalen, Germany

61

William IV Duke of Julich-Berg

b: 09 Jan 1455

m:

d: 06 Sep 1511

75

Maria of Julich-Berg

b: 03 Aug 1491 Jülich, Duren, Nordrhein-Westfalen, Germany

d: 29 Aug 1543

Philip Habsburg I of Castile

b: 22 Jul 1478
Bruges, Gironde,
Aquitaine, France
m:
d: 25 Sep 1506
Burgos, Burgos,
Castilla-Leon,
Spain

Ferdinand I Holy Roman Emperor

b: 10 Mar 1503
Alcalá de Henares,
Madrid, Madrid,
Spain
m:
d: 25 Jul 1564
Vienna, Austria

Joanna Juana La Loca Trastamara

b: 06 Nov 1479 Toledo, Toledo,
Castilla-La Mancha, Spain
d: 13 Apr 1555 Tordesillas,
Valladolid, Castilla-Leon, Spain

Maria Habsburg of Austria

b: 15 May 1531
Wien, Vienna,
Austria
m:
d: 11 Dec 1581
Hambach, Duren,
Nordrhein-
Westfalen,
Germany

61

Anna of Bohemia and Hungary

b: 23 Jul 1503
Praha, Czech
Republic
d: 27 Jan 1547
Praha, Czech
Republic

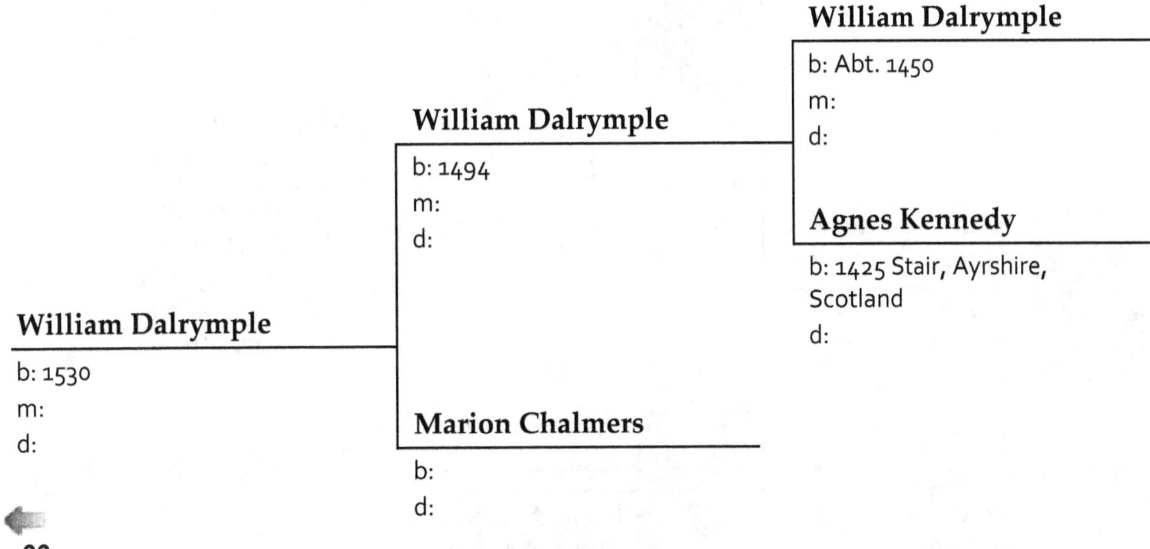

William Dalrymple
b: 1530
m:
d:

66

William Dalrymple
b: 1494
m:
d:

Marion Chalmers
b:
d:

William Dalrymple
b: Abt. 1450
m:
d:

Agnes Kennedy
b: 1425 Stair, Ayrshire, Scotland
d:

Adolph I Duke of Cleves

b: 02 Aug 1373
m: 22 Jul 1406
Dijon, Cote d'Or,
Bourgogne, France
d: 23 Sep 1448

John I Duke of Cleves

b: 16 Feb 1419
m:
d: 05 Sep 1481

Marie of Burgundy Duchess of Cleves

b: 1393 Dijon, Cantal,
Auvergne, France
d: 30 Oct 1463 Kalkar,
Euskirchen, Nordrhein-
Westfalen, Germany

John II Duke of Cleves

b: 1458 Bruxelles,
Brabant, Belgium
m: 1490
d: 1521 Cleve,
Gutersloh,
Nordrhein-
Westfalen,
Germany

Elizabeth Of Nevers

b: 1439 Nevers,
Nievre, Bourgogne,
France
d: 1483 Kleef,
Mettmann,
Nordrhein-
Westfalen,
Germany

71

**Gerhard VII
Duke of Julich-
Berg**

b: 1416
m:
d: 19 Aug 1475

**William IV
Duke of Julich-
Berg**

b: 09 Jan 1455
m:
d: 06 Sep 1511

71

**Philip
Habsburg I of
Castile**

b: 22 Jul 1478
Bruges, Gironde,
Aquitaine, France
m:
d: 25 Sep 1506
Burgos, Burgos,
Castilla-Leon,
Spain

**Maximilian I
Holy Roman
Emperor**

b: 22 Mar 1459
m:
d: 12 Jan 1519

**Frederick III
Holy Roman
Emperor**

b: 21 Sep 1415
m:
d: 19 Aug 1493

72

Adolph I Duke of Cleves

b: 02 Aug 1373
m: 22 Jul 1406
Dijon, Cote d'Or,
Bourgogne, France
d: 23 Sep 1448

74

Adolph III Duke of Cleves

b: 1334
m: 1369
d: 07 Sep 1394 Heiligenstadt,
Altotting, Bayern, Germany

Margaret of Julich

b: 1342 Amberg, Amberg,
Bayern, Germany
d: 1425 Kleve, Rheinland-Pfalz,
Germany

Ancestors of Larry Dan Duffy

Generation 1

1.   **Larry Dan Duffy,** son of Clinton Rex Duffy and Violet Oresta Yoakum was born on 22 Jun 1939 in Centralia, Lewis, Washington. He married **Nancy Joan Krause**, daughter of Franz Henry Krause and Sophie Agnes Koehle on 05 Aug 1967. She was born on 25 Dec 1945 in Chehalis, Lewis, Washington, USA.

Generation 2

2.   **Clinton Rex Duffy,** son of Lloyd Franklin Duffy and Eunice Anderson was born on 05 Feb 1917 in Centralia, Lewis, Washington. He died in Sep 1988 in Chula Vista, San Diego, California. He married **Violet Oresta Yoakum**, daughter of Thomas Ralph Yoakum and Margaret Lyons MacDonald in 1938 in Tacoma, Pierce, Washington.

3.   **Violet Oresta Yoakum,** daughter of Thomas Ralph Yoakum and Margaret Lyons MacDonald was born on 10 Apr 1919 in Tenino, Thurston, Washington. She died on 23 Dec 1990 in Centralia, Lewis, Washington.

Violet Oresta Yoakum and Clinton Rex Duffy had the following child:

 1. i. Larry Dan Duffy, son of Clinton Rex Duffy and Violet Oresta Yoakum was born on 22 Jun 1939 in Centralia, Lewis, Washington. He married Nancy Joan Krause, daughter of Franz Henry Krause and Sophie Agnes Koehle on 05 Aug 1967. She was born on 25 Dec 1945 in Chehalis, Lewis, Washington, USA.

Generation 3

4.   **Lloyd Franklin Duffy,** son of Horatio Joseph Duffy and Norah Ida Bell Long was born on 29 Sep 1889 in Washington. He died on 23 May 1930 in Centralia, Lewis, Washington. He married **Eunice Anderson**, daughter of George Washington Anderson and Amelia Alice Sewall on 26 Jun 1916 in Lewis, Washington.

5.   **Eunice Anderson,** daughter of George Washington Anderson and Amelia Alice Sewall was born in Nov 1897 in Washington. She died on 23 May 1930 in Centralia, Lewis, Washington.

Eunice Anderson and Lloyd Franklin Duffy had the following children:

 2. i. Clinton Rex Duffy, son of Lloyd Franklin Duffy and Eunice Anderson was born on 05 Feb 1917 in Centralia, Lewis, Washington. He died in Sep 1988 in Chula Vista, San Diego, California. He married Violet Oresta Yoakum, daughter of Thomas Ralph Yoakum and Margaret Lyons MacDonald in 1938 in Tacoma, Pierce, Washington. She was born on 10 Apr 1919 in Tenino, Thurston, Washington. She died on 23 Dec 1990 in Centralia, Lewis, Washington. He married Shirley R Lucier on 05 Oct 1971 in Kern, California. She was born about 1927. He married Galena Tikhonoff. She was born on 23 Jun 1924 in San Francisco, San Francisco, California. She died on 21 May 1971 in Chula Vista, San Diego, California.

   ii. Lee Kendall Duffy, son of Lloyd Franklin Duffy and Eunice Anderson was born on 04 Sep 1919 in Lewis, Washington, United States.

6.   **Thomas Ralph Yoakum,** son of Isaac Turner Yoakum and Alice Elizabeth Duncan was born on 03 Jun 1879 in Mount Pleasant, Henry, Iowa. He died on 16 Apr 1942 in Centralia, Lewis,

Washington. He married **Margaret Lyons MacDonald**, daughter of Robert Clark MacDonald and Mary Jane Stevens in 1905.

7.   **Margaret Lyons MacDonald**, daughter of Robert Clark MacDonald and Mary Jane Stevens was born on 11 Jan 1889 in Tatamagouche, Colchester, Nova Scotia, Canada. She died on 19 May 1980 in Centralia, Lewis, Washington.

Margaret Lyons MacDonald and Thomas Ralph Yoakum had the following children:

    i.   Mary Alice Yoakum, daughter of Thomas Ralph Yoakum and Margaret Lyons MacDonald was born on 20 Aug 1906 in Thurston, Washington.

    ii.   Tressa Margaret Yoakum, daughter of Thomas Ralph Yoakum and Margaret Lyons MacDonald was born on 16 Jun 1913 in Thurston, Washington. She died on 21 Feb 1991 in Chehalis, Lewis, Washington. She married Harvey William Barner on 16 Jun 1930 in Centralia, Lewis, Washington. He was born about 1909 in Washington.

    iii.   Aubrey Delmont Yoakum, son of Thomas Ralph Yoakum and Margaret Lyons MacDonald was born in 1910 in Washington.

    iv.   Lillian R Yoakum, daughter of Thomas Ralph Yoakum and Margaret Lyons MacDonald was born on 30 Sep 1907 in Thurston, Washington.

3.   v.   Violet Oresta Yoakum, daughter of Thomas Ralph Yoakum and Margaret Lyons MacDonald was born on 10 Apr 1919 in Tenino, Thurston, Washington. She died on 23 Dec 1990 in Centralia, Lewis, Washington. She married Clinton Rex Duffy, son of Lloyd Franklin Duffy and Eunice Anderson in 1938 in Tacoma, Pierce, Washington. He was born on 05 Feb 1917 in Centralia, Lewis, Washington. He died in Sep 1988 in Chula Vista, San Diego, California. She married Richard Wedmark on 11 Nov 1945 in Centralia, Lewis, Washington. She married George White on 13 Apr 1950 in Centralia, Lewis, Washington. He died in Centralia, Lewis, Washington, USA.

    vi.   Roberta Yoakum, daughter of Thomas Ralph Yoakum and Margaret Lyons MacDonald was born in 1907. She died on 16 Oct 1917 in Olympia, Thurston County, Washington (Age at Death: 10).

Generation 4

8.   **Horatio Joseph Duffy,** son of Bernard Andrew Duffy and Elizabeth "Ely" Hess was born on 19 Jun 1851 in Wheeling, Marshall County, West Virginia. He died on 08 Jan 1927 in Spokane, Washington (Buried at Mountain View Cemetery, Centralia, WA). He married **Norah Ida Bell Long,** daughter of William Henry Long and Socelia Wirick on 03 Nov 1878 in Lewis, Washington.

9.   **Norah Ida Bell Long,** daughter of William Henry Long and Socelia Wirick was born in Jun 1861 in Marion, Henry, Iowa. She died on 05 Jan 1917 in Lewis Washington.

Norah Ida Bell Long and Horatio Joseph Duffy had the following children:

i.   Joseph Lorenzo Duffy, son of Horatio Joseph Duffy and Norah Ida Bell Long was born on 28 Aug 1882 in Lewis County, Washington. He died on 28 Jan 1920 in Moscow, Latah, Idaho buried Centralia Lewis Washington. He married Ada Byers, daughter of Enos Byers and Sarah A. Stephenson on 31 Dec 1902 in Latah County, Idaho. She was born about 1886 in Iowa. She died on 05 Feb 1920 in Moscow, Latah, Idaho, USA (Age: 34).

ii.   Lorenia Belle Duffy, daughter of Horatio Joseph Duffy and Norah Ida Bell Long was born on 08 Apr 1886 in Washington. She died on 19 Nov 1972 in Pierce, Washington. She married Samuel E Butler on 20 Sep 1924 in Pierce, Washington. He was born on 15 Jan 1887 in Michigan. He died on 09 Sep 1965 in Pierce, Washington. She married Late Fronret Dixon, son of Levi Dixon and Mary F Dixon on 14 Jun 1911 in Lewis, Washington. He was born in Aug 1889 in Colorado, USA. He died in 1974 (Age: 85).

iii.   Walter Americus Duffy, son of Horatio Joseph Duffy and Norah Ida Bell Long was born on 06 Jan 1888 in Washington. He died on 27 May 1914 in Poplar Bluff, Butler, Missouri (Died of appendicitis). He married Sarah Faulk on 04 Nov 1912 in Ripley, Missouri. She was born on 17 Aug 1892 in Illinois, United States. She died on 28 Dec 1970 in Modesto, California.

iv.   Thomas Horatio Duffy, son of Horatio Joseph Duffy and Norah Ida Bell Long was born on 06 Jan 1884 in Lewis, Washington. He died on 21 Jul 1960 in Tacoma, Pierce, Washington (Age: 76). He married Florence Dove Whiting on 28 Aug 1943 in Tacoma, Pierce, Washington. She was born in Oxford, Henry, Illinois.

4.   v.   Lloyd Franklin Duffy, son of Horatio Joseph Duffy and Norah Ida Bell Long was born on 29 Sep 1889 in Washington. He died on 23 May 1930 in Centralia, Lewis, Washington. He married Eunice Anderson, daughter of George Washington Anderson and Amelia Alice Sewall on 26 Jun 1916 in Lewis, Washington. She was born in Nov 1897 in Washington. She died on 23 May 1930 in Centralia, Lewis, Washington.

vi.   Lucretia Duffy, daughter of Horatio Joseph Duffy and Norah Ida Bell Long was born on 17 May 1881 in Washington. She died on 07 Aug 1953 in Centralia, Lewis, Washington.

vii.   Maude Edith Duffy, daughter of Horatio Joseph Duffy and Norah Ida Bell Long was born on 18 Aug 1879 in Washington.

10.   **George Washington Anderson**, son of Charles Perry Anderson and Mary Ann Cahoon was born on 24 Feb 1861 in Portland, Multnomah, Oregon. He died on 04 Jan 1946 in Lewis County, Washington. He married **Amelia Alice Sewall**, daughter of Chris Sewall and Rosa in 1896.

11.   **Amelia Alice Sewall**, daughter of Chris Sewall and Rosa was born in Mar 1871 in Washington. She died on 06 Jan 1941 in Lewis.

Amelia Alice Sewall and George Washington Anderson had the following child:

5.   i.   Eunice Anderson, daughter of George Washington Anderson and Amelia Alice
               Sewall was born in Nov 1897 in Washington. She died on 23 May 1930 in
               Centralia, Lewis, Washington. She married Lloyd Franklin Duffy, son of Horatio
               Joseph Duffy and Norah Ida Bell Long on 26 Jun 1916 in Lewis, Washington. He
               was born on 29 Sep 1889 in Washington. He died on 23 May 1930 in Centralia,
               Lewis, Washington.

12.   **Isaac Turner Yoakum**, son of Edward C. Yoakum and Mary Dalrymple Stewart was born on 05
        Feb 1849 in Illinois. He died on 16 Jun 1933 in Tenino, Thurston County, Washington. He
        married **Alice Elizabeth Duncan**, daughter of William T. H. Duncan and Eve Miller on 12 Mar
        1871 in Menard County, Illinois.

13.   **Alice Elizabeth Duncan**, daughter of William T. H. Duncan and Eve Miller was born on 06 Dec
        1850 in Sangamon County, Illinois. She died on 30 Jul 1924 in Olympia, Thurston County,
        Washington.

        Alice Elizabeth Duncan and Isaac Turner Yoakum had the following children:
                i.   Angeline Yoakum, daughter of Isaac Turner Yoakum and Alice Elizabeth Duncan
                       was born on 26 Oct 1883 in Illinois. She died in Centralia, Lewis, Washington.

6.   ii.   Thomas Ralph Yoakum, son of Isaac Turner Yoakum and Alice Elizabeth Duncan
               was born on 03 Jun 1879 in Mount Pleasant, Henry, Iowa. He died on 16 Apr 1942
               in Centralia, Lewis, Washington. He married Margaret Lyons MacDonald,
               daughter of Robert Clark MacDonald and Mary Jane Stevens in 1905. She was
               born on 11 Jan 1889 in Tatamagouche, Colchester, Nova Scotia, Canada. She
               died on 19 May 1980 in Centralia, Lewis, Washington. He married Hattie M
               Yoakum. She was born about 1890 in Missouri.

14.   **Robert Clark MacDonald**, son of Angus MacDonald and Ann Clark was born in 1850 in
        Tatamagouche, Colchester, Nova Scotia, Canada. He died on 16 Mar 1925 in Tenino, Thurston,
        Washington (Buried at the Odd Fellows Cemetery in Olympia, WA). He married **Mary Jane
        Stevens**, daughter of Rany Stevens and Nellie Johnson on 16 Aug 1874 in Bayhead,
        Colchester, Nova Scotia.

15.   **Mary Jane Stevens**, daughter of Rany Stevens and Nellie Johnson was born on 10 Feb 1847 in
        Wallace, Cumberland, Nova Scotia, Canada. She died on 16 Oct 1926 in Centralia, Lewis,
        Washington (Buried at the Odd Fellows Cemetery in Olympia, WA).

        Mary Jane Stevens and Robert Clark MacDonald had the following children:
7.   i.   Margaret Lyons MacDonald, daughter of Robert Clark MacDonald and Mary Jane
               Stevens was born on 11 Jan 1889 in Tatamagouche, Colchester, Nova Scotia,
               Canada. She died on 19 May 1980 in Centralia, Lewis, Washington. She married
               G. Ralph Alverson on 07 Mar 1931 in Olympia, Thurston, Washington. He was
               born on 07 Mar 1878. He died on 16 Apr 1959. She married Thomas Ralph
               Yoakum, son of Isaac Turner Yoakum and Alice Elizabeth Duncan in 1905. He was
               born on 03 Jun 1879 in Mount Pleasant, Henry, Iowa. He died on 16 Apr 1942 in
               Centralia, Lewis, Washington.

        ii.   Harry Weller MacDonald, son of Robert Clark MacDonald and Mary Jane Stevens
               was born on 20 Oct 1878 in Tatamagouche, Colchester, Nova Scotia, Canada. He

died on 30 Apr 1948 (Buried in Merrill, Maine). He married Inez Sybil Gardner. She was born on 22 Dec 1884 in Merrill, Aroostook, Maine. She died on 20 Jul 1971.

iii. Earl Bradford MacDonald, son of Robert Clark MacDonald and Mary Jane Stevens was born about 1875 in Tatamagouche, Colchester, Nova Scotia, Canada. He died in Jan 1952 in Centralia, Lewis, Washington (Age at Death: 75). He married Lilian Elizabeth Small. She was born about 1886 in Smyrna Mills, Aroostook, Maine. She died in Apr 1951 in Centralia, Lewis, Washington.

iv. Anne "Annie" Blanche MacDonald, daughter of Robert Clark MacDonald and Mary Jane Stevens was born on 01 Aug 1880 in Tatamagouche, Colchester, Nova Scotia. She married James Aubrey Vaughn on 20 Nov 1901 in Smyrna Mills, Aroostook, Maine. He was born in 1878 in Nova Scotia, Canada.

v. Nellie May MacDonald, daughter of Robert Clark MacDonald and Mary Jane Stevens was born on 05 Oct 1876 in Tatamagouche, Colchester, Nova Scotia, Canada. She died in 1919 in Tatamagouche, Colchester, Nova Scotia, Canada. She married John Havelock Spinney.

vi. James Isaac MacDonald, son of Robert Clark MacDonald and Mary Jane Stevens was born on 01 Oct 1885 in Tatamagouche, Colchester, Nova Scotia, Canada.

vii. George Wellwood MacDonald, son of Robert Clark MacDonald and Mary Jane Stevens was born on 11 Nov 1882 in Tatamagouche, Colchester, Nova Scotia, Canada. He died in Apr 1963. He married Jennie Webster.

Generation 5

16. **Bernard Andrew Duffy** was born in Aug 1805 in Donegal, Ireland. He died on 08 Sep 1869 in St.Louis, St. Louis Missouri. He married **Elizabeth "Ely" Hess**, daughter of George Henry Hess and Anna Barbara Linhart in 1833 in Pennsylvania.

17. **Elizabeth "Ely" Hess**, daughter of George Henry Hess and Anna Barbara Linhart was born on 05 Aug 1812 in Westmoreland County, Pennsylvania. She died on 22 Feb 1907 in Macon County, Missouri.

Notes for Elizabeth "Ely" Hess:
02-14-2010 02;35;10PM
http://trees.ancestry.com/rd?f=image&guid=78bfb3bc-cac9-4c57-af2d-917c07222f80&tid=251
61444&pid=75

Elizabeth "Ely" Hess and Bernard Andrew Duffy had the following children:
i. Bernard Duffy Jr., son of Bernard Andrew Duffy and Elizabeth "Ely" Hess was born on Jun 1832/1834 in Pennsylvania. He died after 1910 in Marshall West Virginia.

ii. Mary Duffy, daughter of Bernard Andrew Duffy and Elizabeth "Ely" Hess was born in 1837 in Pennsylvania, USA.

iii. Evarilla E. Duffy, daughter of Bernard Andrew Duffy and Elizabeth "Ely" Hess was born in Apr 1846 in West Virginia. She died on 15 Oct 1922 in National City San Diego Co. California.

iv. Franklin Duffy, son of Bernard Andrew Duffy and Elizabeth "Ely" Hess was born in 1853 in Ohio. He died on 16 Sep 1873 in Sacramento, Sacramento, California, USA.

v. Americus Duffy, son of Bernard Andrew Duffy and Elizabeth "Ely" Hess was born in 1856 in Ohio. He died on 08 Jan 1927 in Centralia, Columbia, Pennsylvania, United States.

vi. George Matthew Duffy, son of Bernard Andrew Duffy and Elizabeth "Ely" Hess was born on 07 Jul 1839 in Belmont, Ohio. He died on 27 Sep 1915 in National City, San Diego, CA.

vii. John Duffy, son of Bernard Andrew Duffy and Elizabeth "Ely" Hess was born in 1841 in Virginia, USA. He died on 17 Feb 1931 in Sunnyside, Snohomish, Washington, USA.

viii. Lawson Duffy, son of Bernard Andrew Duffy and Elizabeth "Ely" Hess was born in 1846 in Virginia, USA. He died on 08 Sep 1869 in St Louis, St Louis, Missouri, USA.

ix. Joseph M. Duffy, son of Bernard Andrew Duffy and Elizabeth "Ely" Hess was born on 06 Aug 1849 in Marshall, Virginia. He died on 02 Apr 1896 in Huntington, Cabell, West Virginia. He married Ella M. Smith in 1875 in Macon, Macon, Missouri.

x. Martha Duffy, daughter of Bernard Andrew Duffy and Elizabeth "Ely" Hess was born in 1843 in Virginia, USA.

xi. Abaretta Duffy, daughter of Bernard Andrew Duffy and Elizabeth "Ely" Hess was born in 1844 in Virginia, USA.

8. xii. Horatio Joseph Duffy, son of Bernard Andrew Duffy and Elizabeth "Ely" Hess was born on 19 Jun 1851 in Wheeling, Marshall County, West Virginia. He died on 08 Jan 1927 in Spokane, Washington (Buried at Mountain View Cemetery, Centralia, WA). He married Norah Ida Bell Long, daughter of William Henry Long and Socelia Wirick on 03 Nov 1878 in Lewis, Washington. She was born in Jun 1861 in Marion, Henry, Iowa. She died on 05 Jan 1917 in Lewis Washington.

xiii. Isaac A Duffy, son of Bernard Andrew Duffy and Elizabeth "Ely" Hess was born on 12 Jan 1860 in Belmont County, Ohio, USA.

18. **William Henry Long**, son of William Long and Rebekah Morrison Suddick was born on 25 Nov 1824 in Franklin, Ohio. He died on 10 Feb 1892 in Chehalis, Lewis, Washington.

19. **Socelia Wirick**, daughter of Jacob Weirich Weirig and Magdalene R was born on 28 Mar 1827 in Lebanon, Pennsylvania. She died on 12 Dec 1868 in Henry County, Iowa (Buried at Oak Grove Cemetery in Mt. Pleasant, Henry County, Iowa).

Socelia Wirick and William Henry Long had the following children:

i. Charles Wesley Long, son of William Henry Long and Socelia Wirick was born in Apr 1856 in Ohio, USA. He died on 25 Oct 1927 in Chehalis, Lewis, Washington, United States. He married Sarah A. Boyd. She was born in 1859 in Iowa. She died on 07 Mar 1936 in Chehalis, Lewis County, Washington.

ii. Mary Anne Long, daughter of William Henry Long and Socelia Wirick was born in 1855 in Iowa, United States.

iii. Joseph R Long, son of William Henry Long and Socelia Wirick was born in 1853 in Iowa, United States.

iv. Martha Matilda Long, daughter of William Henry Long and Socelia Wirick was born on 03 May 1850 in Franklin Ohio. She died on 24 Feb 1893 in Lewis, Washington. She married Sanford M Black on 27 Feb 1868 in Trenton, Henry, Iowa. He was born in Apr 1848 in Trenton, Henry, Iowa. He died on 21 Feb 1919 in Tacoma, Pierce, Washington.

v. Thomas Jefferson Long, son of William Henry Long and Socelia Wirick was born in Jun 1864 in Council Bluffs, Iowa. He died on 18 Oct 1931 in Chehalis, Lewis, Washington. He married Minnie Sherman Grove. She was born on 25 Nov 1867 in Shelby, Edwards, Illinois. She died on 20 Nov 1958 in Chehalis, Lewis, Washington.

vi. James Solomon Long, son of William Henry Long and Socelia Wirick was born on 11 Oct 1858 in Henry, Iowa. He died on 14 Mar 1912 in Chehalis, Lewis, Washington (Age at Death: 53).

9. vii. Norah Ida Bell Long, daughter of William Henry Long and Socelia Wirick was born in Jun 1861 in Marion, Henry, Iowa. She died on 05 Jan 1917 in Lewis Washington. She married John T Campbel in 1899. He was born in Dec 1862 in Canada Eng. She married Horatio Joseph Duffy, son of Bernard Andrew Duffy and Elizabeth "Ely" Hess on 03 Nov 1878 in Lewis, Washington. He was born on 19 Jun 1851 in Wheeling, Marshall County, West Virginia. He died on 08 Jan 1927 in Spokane, Washington (Buried at Mountain View Cemetery, Centralia, WA).

viii. George William Long, son of William Henry Long and Socelia Wirick was born in 1849 in Franklin, Ohio. He died on 12 Sep 1920 in Chehalis, Lewis, Washington (Age: 71). He married Emily E Long in 1871. She was born in Jul 1853 in Iowa.

ix. Sarah C Long, daughter of William Henry Long and Socelia Wirick was born in

1847 in Ohio.

    x.   John Henry Long, son of William Henry Long and Socelia Wirick was born on 27 Nov 1845 in Columbus, Franklin, Ohio. He died on 21 Jan 1898 in Chehalis, Lewis, Washington (Age: 52). He married Deborah W. Hodgon in 1868. She was born in 1850 in Massachusetts, USA. She died on 07 Mar 1892 in El Paso, El Paso, Texas, USA. He married Henrietta Steward on 01 Mar 1893. She was born in Indianna.

    xi.   Andrew Jackson Long, son of William Henry Long and Socelia Wirick was born in Sep 1868 in Henry County, Iowa. He died on 27 Jun 1926 in Olympia, Thurston, Washington (Age: 58). He married Katherine Amelia Grove. She was born on 28 Aug 1869 in Prairie Home, Illinois. She died on 17 Oct 1962 in Olympia, Thurston, Washington (Age: 93).

20.   **Charles Perry Anderson**, son of James Anderson and Elizabeth Clifton was born on 24 Mar 1825 in Kentucky. He died on 23 Sep 1905 in Centralia, Lewis, Washington. He married **Mary Ann Cahoon** on 16 Mar 1851 in Nodaway, Missouri.

21.   **Mary Ann Cahoon** was born on 14 Dec 1829 in Ohio. She died on 01 Jun 1902 in Centralia, Lewis, Washington.

Mary Ann Cahoon and Charles Perry Anderson had the following children:

10.   i.   George Washington Anderson, son of Charles Perry Anderson and Mary Ann Cahoon was born on 24 Feb 1861 in Portland, Multnomah, Oregon. He died on 04 Jan 1946 in Lewis County, Washington. He married Amelia Alice Sewall, daughter of Chris Sewall and Rosa in 1896. She was born in Mar 1871 in Washington. She died on 06 Jan 1941 in Lewis. He married Clara Ticknor in 1890. She was born in 1872. She died in 1893 in Bucoda, Thurston, Washington, USA.

    ii.   Minnie Anderson, daughter of Charles Perry Anderson and Mary Ann Cahoon was born in 1870 in Oregon.

    iii.   Charles T. Anderson, son of Charles Perry Anderson and Mary Ann Cahoon was born in 1856 in Washington County, Oregon, USA.

    iv.   John A Anderson, son of Charles Perry Anderson and Mary Ann Cahoon was born in 1854 in Oregon.

    v.   Eliza J Anderson, daughter of Charles Perry Anderson and Mary Ann Cahoon was born in 1862 in Oregon.

    vi.   Annie Anderson, daughter of Charles Perry Anderson and Mary Ann Cahoon was born about 1872 in Washington Territory.

22.   **Chris Sewall** was born on 25 Dec 1828 in Prussia. He died on 25 Nov 1895 in Centralia, Lewis, Washington.

23.   **Rosa** was born on 23 Mar 1829 in Prussia. She died on 28 Oct 1911 in Centralia, Lewis,

Washington.

Rosa and Chris Sewall had the following children:

    i.   Louis Sewall, son of Chris Sewall and Rosa was born in 1863 in Iowa. He died in 1939.

    ii.   August "Ikey" Sewall, son of Chris Sewall and Rosa was born in 1869 in Washington Territory.

11.   iii.   Amelia Alice Sewall, daughter of Chris Sewall and Rosa was born in Mar 1871 in Washington. She died on 06 Jan 1941 in Lewis. She married George Washington Anderson, son of Charles Perry Anderson and Mary Ann Cahoon in 1896. He was born on 24 Feb 1861 in Portland, Multnomah, Oregon. He died on 04 Jan 1946 in Lewis County, Washington.

24.   **Edward C. Yoakum**, son of James Yoakum and Julia Owens was born on 02 Mar 1814 in Claiborne County, Tennessee. He died in 1869 in Menard County, Illinois. He married **Mary Dalrymple Stewart**, daughter of Rev. William McCallen Stewart and Ann Laughlin on 04 Jul 1839 in Muscatine, Muscatine, Iowa.

25.   **Mary Dalrymple Stewart**, daughter of Rev. William McCallen Stewart and Ann Laughlin was born on 20 Feb 1825 in Bond, Illinois. She died on 21 Jun 1909 in Tenino, Thurston, Washington.

Mary Dalrymple Stewart and Edward C. Yoakum had the following children:

    i.   Martha Ann Yoakum, daughter of Edward C. Yoakum and Mary Dalrymple Stewart was born on 15 Dec 1845 in Iowa. She died on 15 Mar 1932 in Tenino, Thurston, Washington (Age at Death: 86). She married Lafayette Davis in 1875. He was born about 1877 in Washington.

    ii.   John Edward Yoakum, son of Edward C. Yoakum and Mary Dalrymple Stewart was born on 04 Nov 1858 in Jasper County, Iowa. He died on 03 May 1950 in Centralia, Lewis, Washington (Age at Death: 91). He married Emma D Mize in 1883. She was born on 23 Aug 1862 in Thurston, Washington. She died on 22 Oct 1941 in Seattle, King, Washington.

12.   iii.   Isaac Turner Yoakum, son of Edward C. Yoakum and Mary Dalrymple Stewart was born on 05 Feb 1849 in Illinois. He died on 16 Jun 1933 in Tenino, Thurston County, Washington. He married Alice Elizabeth Duncan, daughter of William T. H. Duncan and Eve Miller on 12 Mar 1871 in Menard County, Illinois. She was born on 06 Dec 1850 in Sangamon County, Illinois. She died on 30 Jul 1924 in Olympia, Thurston County, Washington.

26.   **William T. H. Duncan,** son of Marshall Duncan and Rachel Thrasher was born on 10 May 1807 in Cumberland County, Kentucky. He died on 20 Oct 1862 in Salisbury, Sangamon County, Illinois. He married **Eve Miller**, daughter of Solomon Miller and Nancy Ann Antle on 08 Dec 1831 in Sangamon County, Illinois.

27.   **Eve Miller,** daughter of Solomon Miller and Nancy Ann Antle was born on 11 Dec 1813 in Adair

County, Kentucky. She died on 17 Apr 1895 in Salisbury, Sangamon County, Illinois.

Eve Miller and William T. H. Duncan had the following children:

i. Marion Miller Duncan, son of William T. H. Duncan and Eve Miller was born on 17 Dec 1832 in Salisbury, Sangamon, Illinois, USA. He died on 14 Oct 1908 in Salisbury, Sangamon, Illinois, USA.

ii. James T Duncan, son of William T. H. Duncan and Eve Miller was born in 1833 in Salisbury, Sangamon, Illinois, USA. He died in 1930 in USA.

iii. Simeon S Duncan, son of William T. H. Duncan and Eve Miller was born in Oct 1836 in Salisbury, Sangamon, Illinois, USA. He died on 31 Jul 1917 in Menard, Illinois, USA.

iv. Polly Mary Ann Duncan, daughter of William T. H. Duncan and Eve Miller was born in Aug 1835 in Salisbury, Sangamon, Illinois. She died on 13 Mar 1909 in Carrollton, Carroll, Missouri.

13. v. Alice Elizabeth Duncan, daughter of William T. H. Duncan and Eve Miller was born on 06 Dec 1850 in Sangamon County, Illinois. She died on 30 Jul 1924 in Olympia, Thurston County, Washington. She married Isaac Turner Yoakum, son of Edward C. Yoakum and Mary Dalrymple Stewart on 12 Mar 1871 in Menard County, Illinois. He was born on 05 Feb 1849 in Illinois. He died on 16 Jun 1933 in Tenino, Thurston County, Washington.

vi. Martha A Duncan, daughter of William T. H. Duncan and Eve Miller was born on 28 Apr 1840 in Salisbury, Sangamon, Illinois. She died in 1930.

vii. Sarah Jane Duncan, daughter of William T. H. Duncan and Eve Miller was born in Nov 1838 in Sangamon, Illinois. She died in Springfield, Sangamon, Illinois.

viii. George W Duncan, son of William T. H. Duncan and Eve Miller was born in May 1843 in Salisbury, Sangamon, Illinois, USA. He died in 1930 in USA.

ix. Margaret S Duncan, daughter of William T. H. Duncan and Eve Miller was born on 28 Nov 1841 in Salisbury, Sangamon, Illinois, USA. She died on 16 Sep 1922 in Salisbury, Sangamon, Illinois, USA.

x. Farinda Osborn Duncan, daughter of William T. H. Duncan and Eve Miller was born in Sep 1846 in Salisbury, Sangamon, Illinois, USA. She died in 1931 in USA.

xi. Nancy Ellen Duncan, daughter of William T. H. Duncan and Eve Miller was born in 1843 in Salisbury, Sangamon, Illinois. She died on 12 Sep 1879 in Sangamon County, Illinois.

xii. Thomas Saskett Duncan, son of William T. H. Duncan and Eve Miller was born on 31 May 1854 in Salisbury, Sangamon, Illinois, USA. He died on 05 Oct 1930 in USA.

28. **Angus MacDonald**, son of Hugh MacDonald and Mary ? was born on 15 Apr 1822 in Tatamagouche, Colchester, Nova Scotia, Canada. He died on 03 Jul 1906 in Tatamagouche Nova Scotia, Canada (Buried in Tatamagouche, Nova Scotia).

29. **Ann Clark** was born in 1822. She died on 15 Aug 1898 in Tatamagouche, Nova Scotia, Canada (Buried in Tatamagouche, Nova Scotia).

Ann Clark and Angus MacDonald had the following children:

14.   i.   Robert Clark MacDonald, son of Angus MacDonald and Ann Clark was born in 1850 in Tatamagouche, Colchester, Nova Scotia, Canada. He died on 16 Mar 1925 in Tenino, Thurston, Washington (Buried at the Odd Fellows Cemetery in Olympia, WA). He married Mary Jane Stevens, daughter of Rany Stevens and Nellie Johnson on 16 Aug 1874 in Bayhead, Colchester, Nova Scotia. She was born on 10 Feb 1847 in Wallace, Cumberland, Nova Scotia, Canada. She died on 16 Oct 1926 in Centralia, Lewis, Washington (Buried at the Odd Fellows Cemetery in Olympia, WA).

   ii.   Janet MacDonald, daughter of Angus MacDonald and Ann Clark was born in 1856 in Tatamagouche, Nova Scotia, Canada.

   iii.   Margaret Ann MacDonald, daughter of Angus MacDonald and Ann Clark was born on 30 Mar 1854 in Tatamagouche, Nova Scotia, Canada. She died on 21 Jan 1884 in Newton Centre, Middlesex, Massachusetts.

   iv.   John George MacDonald, son of Angus MacDonald and Ann Clark was born on 04 Jul 1852 in Tatamagouche Nova Scotia, Canada. He died on 30 May 1941.

   v.   Mary MacDonald, daughter of Angus MacDonald and Ann Clark was born on 04 Feb 1847 in Tatamagouche Nova Scotia, Canada.

30. **Rany Stevens**.

31. **Nellie Johnson**.

Nellie Johnson and Rany Stevens had the following child:

15.   i.   Mary Jane Stevens, daughter of Rany Stevens and Nellie Johnson was born on 10 Feb 1847 in Wallace, Cumberland, Nova Scotia, Canada. She died on 16 Oct 1926 in Centralia, Lewis, Washington (Buried at the Odd Fellows Cemetery in Olympia, WA). She married Robert Clark MacDonald, son of Angus MacDonald and Ann Clark on 16 Aug 1874 in Bayhead, Colchester, Nova Scotia. He was born in 1850 in Tatamagouche, Colchester, Nova Scotia, Canada. He died on 16 Mar 1925 in Tenino, Thurston, Washington (Buried at the Odd Fellows Cemetery in Olympia, WA).

Generation 6

34. **George Henry Hess** was born on 09 Jun 1780 in Maryland. He died on 27 Oct 1868 in Ashland, Clarion, Pennsylvania. He married **Anna Barbara Linhart**, daughter of John Adam Linhart and Maria Sara Baughman on 31 Oct 1808 in Herkimer or Montgomery, NY.

35. **Anna Barbara Linhart**, daughter of John Adam Linhart and Maria Sara Baughman was born on 03 Feb 1785 in Pennsylvania. She died on 27 Jul 1866 in Ashland, Clarion, Pennsylvania.

Anna Barbara Linhart and George Henry Hess had the following children:

    i. William Hess.

    ii. John George Hess, son of George Henry Hess and Anna Barbara Linhart was born on 03 Jun 1811 in Bush Creek Lutheran, Westmoreland, PA.

    iii. Martha Hess.

17.   iv. Elizabeth "Ely" Hess, daughter of George Henry Hess and Anna Barbara Linhart was born on 05 Aug 1812 in Westmoreland County, Pennsylvania. She died on 22 Feb 1907 in Macon County, Missouri. She married Bernard Andrew Duffy in 1833 in Pennsylvania. He was born in Aug 1805 in Donegal, Ireland. He died on 08 Sep 1869 in St.Louis, St. Louis Missouri.

    v. Issac Layton Hess, son of George Henry Hess and Anna Barbara Linhart was born on 01 Feb 1810 in Bush Creek Lutheran, Westmoreland, PA. He died on 29 Aug 1879 in Clarion Co PA, Ashland, Kossuth.

36. **William Long,** son of William M Long and Margaret Archibald was born on 24 Jan 1781 in Colchester, Nova Scotia, Canada. He died on 09 Jan 1851 in Columbus, Ohio. He married **Rebekah Morrison Suddick** on 16 Jun 1813 in Franklin, Ohio.

37. **Rebekah Morrison Suddick** was born on 10 Jul 1790 in Nova Scotia, Canada. She died on 22 Jan 1864 in Columbus, Franklin, Ohio.

Rebekah Morrison Suddick and William Long had the following child:

18.   i. William Henry Long, son of William Long and Rebekah Morrison Suddick was born on 25 Nov 1824 in Franklin, Ohio. He died on 10 Feb 1892 in Chehalis, Lewis, Washington. She was born on 28 Mar 1827 in Lebanon, Pennsylvania. She died on 12 Dec 1868 in Henry County, Iowa (Buried at Oak Grove Cemetery in Mt. Pleasant, Henry County, Iowa). He married Vienna in 1880. He married Mary Murray in 1886 in Portland, Multnomah, Oregon. He married Susan East in 1889. She was born on 10 Mar 1839 in Morgan County, Missouri. She died on 13 Nov 1925 in Orting, Pierce, Washington.

38. **Jacob Weirich Weirig**. He married **Magdalene R.**

39. **Magdalene R**.

Magdalene R and Jacob Weirich Weirig had the following child:

19.   i. Socelia Wirick, daughter of Jacob Weirich Weirig and Magdalene R was born on 28 Mar 1827 in Lebanon, Pennsylvania. She died on 12 Dec 1868 in Henry County, Iowa (Buried at Oak Grove Cemetery in Mt. Pleasant, Henry County, Iowa). He was born on 25 Nov 1824 in Franklin, Ohio. He died on 10 Feb 1892 in Chehalis, Lewis, Washington.

40. **James Anderson** was born about 1802. He died on 25 Jun 1852. He married **Elizabeth Clifton.**

41. **Elizabeth Clifton**, daughter of John Clifton was born on 02 Apr 1803 in Indianna. She died in 1902.

Elizabeth Clifton and James Anderson had the following child:

20.   i.   Charles Perry Anderson, son of James Anderson and Elizabeth Clifton was born on 24 Mar 1825 in Kentucky. He died on 23 Sep 1905 in Centralia, Lewis, Washington. He married Mary Ann Cahoon on 16 Mar 1851 in Nodaway, Missouri. She was born on 14 Dec 1829 in Ohio. She died on 01 Jun 1902 in Centralia, Lewis, Washington.

48. **James Yoakum**, son of George Washington Yoakum Sr. and Martha Van Bibber was born in 1787 in Greenbrier County, West Virginia. He died in 1834 in Menard County, Illinois. He married **Julia Owens**, daughter of William Owens and Elizabeth Meffin in 1810 in Claiborne County, Tennessee.

49. **Julia Owens**, daughter of William Owens and Elizabeth Meffin was born in 1787 in Claiborne, Tennessee. She died in 1832 in Menard County, Illinois.

Julia Owens and James Yoakum had the following children:

   i.   William Yoakum, son of James Yoakum and Julia Owens was born on 28 Jul 1812 in Claiborne County, Tennessee. He died in Illinois. He married Priscilla Batterton, daughter of Amor Amos Batterton and Nancy Guthrie on 06 Jun 1836 in Sangamon County, Illinois. She was born on 09 Feb 1809 in Kentucky. She died on 16 Mar 1876 in Salisbury, Sangamon County, Illinois.

24.   ii.   Edward C. Yoakum, son of James Yoakum and Julia Owens was born on 02 Mar 1814 in Claiborne County, Tennessee. He died in 1869 in Menard County, Illinois. He married Mary Dalrymple Stewart, daughter of Rev. William McCallen Stewart and Ann Laughlin on 04 Jul 1839 in Muscatine, Muscatine, Iowa. She was born on 20 Feb 1825 in Bond, Illinois. She died on 21 Jun 1909 in Tenino, Thurston, Washington.

   iii.   John H. Yoakum, son of James Yoakum and Julia Owens was born on 15 Oct 1815 in Montgomery County, Illinois. He died on 07 Jun 1885 in Athens, Menard County, Illinois. He married Nancy West on 11 Aug 1839 in Menard County, Illinois.

   iv.   Elizabeth Yoakum, daughter of James Yoakum and Julia Owens was born on 18 Aug 1817 in Montgomery County, Illinois. She died in 1874.

   v.   Martha Yoakum, daughter of James Yoakum and Julia Owens was born on 19 Jun 1819 in Madison County, Illinois. She died in 1874.

   vi.   Isaac Newton Yoakum, son of James Yoakum and Julia Owens was born on 31 Dec 1820 in Madison County, Illinois. He died on 25 Mar 1885 in Red Rock, Marion, Iowa (Age: 64). He married Caroline Wiseman on 15 Dec 1842 in Sangamon, Illinois. She was born in Dec 1822 in Crawford County, Indiana. She died on 07 Oct 1907 in Marion County, Iowa.

vii. James Nelson Yoakum, son of James Yoakum and Julia Owens was born on 12 Aug 1822 in Menard County, Illinois. He died on 18 Oct 1846 in Camargo, Mexico (Died in Mexican American War).

viii. Fanny Yoakum, daughter of James Yoakum and Julia Owens was born on 16 Jul 1825 in Menard County, Illinois. She died in 1874.

ix. George A. Yoakum, son of James Yoakum and Julia Owens was born on 12 Mar 1826 in Menard County, Illinois, United States. He died on 23 Apr 1847 in Cerro Gordo, Mexico (Died in Mexican American War).

x. Nancy Ann Yoakum, daughter of James Yoakum and Julia Owens was born on 04 Nov 1827 in Menard County, Illinois, United States. She died in 1874.

xi. Benjamin Yoakum, son of James Yoakum and Julia Owens was born on 09 Jan 1830 in Menard County, Illinois. He died in 1874.

xii. Judy Yoakum, daughter of James Yoakum and Julia Owens was born on 03 Mar 1832 in Menard County, Illinois. She died in 1874.

50. **Rev. William McCallen Stewart**, son of Rev. Robert Stewart Sr. and Margaret McCallen was born on 24 Apr 1794 in On the Monongahela River, near Brownsville, Fayette, Pennsylvania (William was born on a flat boat as his parents Robert and Ann (Park) Stewart were emigrating to Kentucky. They landed in Kentucky at the place where Frankfort is now located. When they landed at the place of destination, William was only 6 days old.). He died on 12 Nov 1885 in Puyallup, Pierce, Washington. He married **Ann Laughlin**, daughter of John Laughlin Jr. and Mary Dalrymple on 22 Feb 1816 in Adams, Ohio.

51. **Ann Laughlin**, daughter of John Laughlin Jr. and Mary Dalrymple was born on 21 May 1795 in Pendleton, Anderson, South Carolina. She died on 23 Mar 1847 in Cedar Rapids, Linn, Iowa (Buried in Brockman Cemetery, Cedar Rapids, Linn County, Iowa).

Notes for Rev. William McCallen Stewart:
William McCallen Stewart (2)
http://trees.ancestry.com/rd?f=image&guid=37297326-ec29-474d-a75b-4ed19760d042&tid=25
161444&pid=119

Ann Laughlin and Rev. William McCallen Stewart had the following children:

25. i. Mary Dalrymple Stewart, daughter of Rev. William McCallen Stewart and Ann Laughlin was born on 20 Feb 1825 in Bond, Illinois. She died on 21 Jun 1909 in Tenino, Thurston, Washington. She married Edward C. Yoakum, son of James Yoakum and Julia Owens on 04 Jul 1839 in Muscatine, Muscatine, Iowa. He was born on 02 Mar 1814 in Claiborne County, Tennessee. He died in 1869 in Menard County, Illinois.

ii. Mildred Durley Stewart, daughter of Rev. William McCallen Stewart and Ann Laughlin was born on 10 Aug 1833 in Putnam, Illinois. She died on 02 Jul 1921 in

Olympia, Pierce, Washington (Age at Death: 87).

iii. William Addison Stewart, son of Rev. William McCallen Stewart and Ann Laughlin was born on 23 Nov 1835 in Putnam, Putnam, Illinois. He died on 09 May 1900 in Harpster, Idaho, Idaho.

iv. James Harvey Stewart, son of Rev. William McCallen Stewart and Ann Laughlin was born on 11 Jan 1838 in Putnam, Illinois. He died on 05 Aug 1919 in Corvallis, Benton, Oregon.

v. James Laughlin Stewart, son of Rev. William McCallen Stewart and Ann Laughlin was born in 1824 in South Carolina, United States.

vi. Samuel Wilson Stewart, son of Rev. William McCallen Stewart and Ann Laughlin was born on 16 Dec 1816 in Eagle Creek, Adams, Ohio. He died on 12 May 1900 in ??.

vii. Margaret McCallen Stewart, daughter of Rev. William McCallen Stewart and Ann Laughlin was born on 20 Oct 1819 in Brown, Ohio. She died on 05 May 1893 in Olympia, Thurston, Washington (Age at Death: 73).

viii. Robert Park Stewart, son of Rev. William McCallen Stewart and Ann Laughlin was born on 20 Apr 1821 in Bond, Illinois. He died in 1911 in ??.

ix. John Laughlin Stewart, son of Rev. William McCallen Stewart and Ann Laughlin was born on 28 Feb 1823 in Bond, Illinois. He died in 1894 in ?.

x. Nancy Ann Stewart, daughter of Rev. William McCallen Stewart and Ann Laughlin was born on 04 Feb 1827 in Greenville, Bond, Illinois. She died on 30 Jul 1907 in Bedford, Taylor, Iowa (Age at Death: 80).

xi. Abraham Williamson Stewart, son of Rev. William McCallen Stewart and Ann Laughlin was born on 10 Dec 1829 in Bond, Illinois. He died on 10 Sep 1910 in Sumner, Pierce, Washington (Age at Death: 80).

xii. Eliza Jane Stewart, daughter of Rev. William McCallen Stewart and Ann Laughlin was born on 15 Dec 1830 in Greenville, Bond, Illinois. She died on 26 Nov 1913 in Puyallup, Pierce, Washington (Age at Death: 82).

52. **Marshall Duncan,** son of James Duncan and Averilla "Ava" Shelton was born in 1783 in Stokes, North Carolina. He died on 03 Dec 1858 in Salisbury, Sangamon, Illinois. He married **Rachel Thrasher**.

53. **Rachel Thrasher,** daughter of William Thrasher and Sarah Elizabeth Phillips was born on 03 Aug 1785 in Kentucky.

Rachel Thrasher and Marshall Duncan had the following children:

26. i. William T. H. Duncan, son of Marshall Duncan and Rachel Thrasher was born on

10 May 1807 in Cumberland County, Kentucky. He died on 20 Oct 1862 in
Salisbury, Sangamon County, Illinois. He married Eve Miller, daughter of
Solomon Miller and Nancy Ann Antle on 08 Dec 1831 in Sangamon County,
Illinois. She was born on 11 Dec 1813 in Adair County, Kentucky. She died on 17
Apr 1895 in Salisbury, Sangamon County, Illinois.

    ii.   Marshall T Duncan, son of Marshall Duncan and Rachel Thrasher was born on 27
Dec 1809 in Cumberland, Harlan, Kentucky, USA. He died on 23 Aug 1840 in
Sangamon, Illinois, USA.

    iii.   James T H Duncan, son of Marshall Duncan and Rachel Thrasher was born on 10
May 1807 in Cumberland County, Kentucky, USA. He died on 09 Jul 1856 in
Salisbury, Sangamon, Illinois.

54.   **Solomon Miller**, son of George Miller and Elizabeth Beaxton was born on 11 May 1796 in
Adair, Kentucky. He died on 07 Jun 1857 in Salisbury, Sangamon, Illinois. He married **Nancy
Ann Antle**, daughter of Henry Antle Sr. and Mary "Polly" Abrell on 13 Aug 1813 in Adair
County, Kentucky.

55.   **Nancy Ann Antle**, daughter of Henry Antle Sr. and Mary "Polly" Abrell was born on 26 Dec
1792 in Lincoln, Kentucky. She died on 01 Apr 1854 in Salisbury, Sangamon, Illinois.

Nancy Ann Antle and Solomon Miller had the following children:

    i.   Nancy Ann Miller, daughter of Solomon Miller and Nancy Ann Antle was born on
18 Dec 1827 in Sangamon, Illinois, United States. She died on 29 Jan 1908 in
Springfield, Sangamon, Illinois, United States.

27.   ii.   Eve Miller, daughter of Solomon Miller and Nancy Ann Antle was born on 11 Dec
1813 in Adair County, Kentucky. She died on 17 Apr 1895 in Salisbury, Sangamon
County, Illinois. She married William T. H. Duncan, son of Marshall Duncan and
Rachel Thrasher on 08 Dec 1831 in Sangamon County, Illinois. He was born on 10
May 1807 in Cumberland County, Kentucky. He died on 20 Oct 1862 in Salisbury,
Sangamon County, Illinois.

    iii.   John Antle Miller, son of Solomon Miller and Nancy Ann Antle was born on 08
Apr 1822 in Salisbury, Sangamon County, Illinois. He died on 02 Nov 1899 in
Salisbury, Sangamon County, Illinois. He married Elizabeth Antle. She was born
in 1781 in Frederick, Virginia, United States. She died in 1870 in Sangamon,
Illinois, United States.

    iv.   George Washington Miller, son of Solomon Miller and Nancy Ann Antle was born
on 18 May 1833 in Salisbury, Sangamon County, Illinois. He died on 27 Oct 1908
in Salisbury, Sangamon County, Illinois. He married M. E..

56.   **Hugh MacDonald**, son of Roderick MacDonald and ? Christian was born in 1795 in Scotland.
He died on 06 Oct 1860 in Wallace Harbor, Nova Scotia, Canada (He apparently drowned in
Wallace Harbour (Cumberland County) while attempting to board a schooner. A short
newspaper article about the incident (dated November 3, 1860) states that the body had yet to
be recovered, and that anyone finding it will "confer a). He married **Mary ?**.

57.   **Mary ?.**

Mary ? and Hugh MacDonald had the following children:

28.   i.   Angus MacDonald, son of Hugh MacDonald and Mary ? was born on 15 Apr 1822 in Tatamagouche, Colchester, Nova Scotia, Canada. He died on 03 Jul 1906 in Tatamagouche Nova Scotia, Canada (Buried in Tatamagouche, Nova Scotia). She was born in 1822. She died on 15 Aug 1898 in Tatamagouche, Nova Scotia, Canada (Buried in Tatamagouche, Nova Scotia).

ii.   Christy MacDonald, daughter of Hugh MacDonald and Mary ? was born in 1832.

iii.   John MacDonald, son of Hugh MacDonald and Mary ? was born in 1826.

iv.   Ann MacDonald, daughter of Hugh MacDonald and Mary ? was born in 1820.

v.   Murdoch MacDonald, son of Hugh MacDonald and Mary ? was born on 11 Feb 1827 in Tatamagouche Nova Scotia, Canada. He died on 30 Jan 1906 in Tatamagouche Nova Scotia, Canada.

vi.   Roderick MacDonald, son of Hugh MacDonald and Mary ? was born on 11 Jul 1820 in Tatamagouche Nova Scotia, Canada. He died on 23 Aug 1884 in Tatamagouche Nova Scotia, Canada.

vii.   Margaret MacDonald, daughter of Hugh MacDonald and Mary ? was born in 1833.

viii.   George MacDonald, son of Hugh MacDonald and Mary ? was born in 1824.

Generation 7

70.   **John Adam Linhart**, son of Christian Lenhart and Anna Maria Heindler was born in 1765 in York, York, Pennsylvania. He died on 05 Jul 1848 in Wilkins, Alleghany, Pennsylvania. He married **Maria Sara Baughman**, daughter of Heinrich Baughman Jr. and Anna Catherina Kunkle in 1794 in Pitt, Allegheny, Pennsylvania.

71.   **Maria Sara Baughman**, daughter of Heinrich Baughman Jr. and Anna Catherina Kunkle was born on 06 Jun 1771 in Upper Hanover, Montgomery, Pennsylvania. She died in 1827 in Wilkins, Alleghany, Pennsylvania.

Maria Sara Baughman and John Adam Linhart had the following children:

i.   John Henry Linhart, son of John Adam Linhart and Maria Sara Baughman was born on 27 Jun 1794 in Allegheny, Pennsylvania, United States.

ii.   Christian Christopher Linhart, son of John Adam Linhart and Maria Sara Baughman was born on 17 Dec 1800 in Allegheny, Pennsylvania, United States. He died on 15 Apr 1870.

iii.   Michael Linhart, son of John Adam Linhart and Maria Sara Baughman was born

on 01 Jan 1799 in Allegheny, Pennsylvania, United States. He died in 1850 in
Allegheny, Pennsylvania, United States.

35.   iv.   Anna Barbara Linhart, daughter of John Adam Linhart and Maria Sara Baughman
was born on 03 Feb 1785 in Pennsylvania. She died on 27 Jul 1866 in Ashland,
Clarion, Pennsylvania. She married George Henry Hess on 31 Oct 1808 in
Herkimer or Montgomery, NY. He was born on 09 Jun 1780 in Maryland. He died
on 27 Oct 1868 in Ashland, Clarion, Pennsylvania.

v.   Catherine Linhart, daughter of John Adam Linhart and Maria Sara Baughman
was born on 29 Aug 1810 in Allegheny, Pennsylvania, United States.

vi.   Esther Linhart, daughter of John Adam Linhart and Maria Sara Baughman was
born on 06 Apr 1803 in Allegheny, Pennsylvania, United States.

vii.   Peter Linhart, son of John Adam Linhart and Maria Sara Baughman was born on
22 Mar 1805 in Westmoreland, Pennsylvania, United States. He died on 28 Apr
1878 in Patton, Allegheny, Pennsylvania, United States.

viii.   Adam Linhart, son of John Adam Linhart and Maria Sara Baughman was born on
28 Nov 1806 in Pittsburg, Allegheny, Pennsylvania, United States. He died on 30
Oct 1889 in Browning, Linn, Missouri, United States.

ix.   Maria Sara Linhart, daughter of John Adam Linhart and Maria Sara Baughman
was born on 17 Oct 1808 in Allegheny, Pennsylvania, United States.

72.   **William M Long** was born on 20 Jul 1744 in Medford, Middlesex, Massachusetts. He died on 08
Apr 1824 in Chillicothe, Ross, Ohio. He married **Margaret Archibald** in 1777 in Colchester, Nova
Scotia, Canad.

73.   **Margaret Archibald** was born in 1760 in Truro, Rockingham, New Hampshire. She died on 02
May 1799 in Chilicothe, Ross, Ohio.

Margaret Archibald and William M Long had the following child:

36.   i.   William Long, son of William M Long and Margaret Archibald was born on 24 Jan
1781 in Colchester, Nova Scotia, Canada. He died on 09 Jan 1851 in Columbus,
Ohio. He married Rebekah Morrison Suddick on 16 Jun 1813 in Franklin, Ohio.
She was born on 10 Jul 1790 in Nova Scotia, Canada. She died on 22 Jan 1864 in
Columbus, Franklin, Ohio.

82.   **John Clifton** was born in Deleware.

John Clifton had the following child:

41.   i.   Elizabeth Clifton, daughter of John Clifton was born on 02 Apr 1803 in Indianna.
She died in 1902. She married James Anderson. He was born about 1802. He
died on 25 Jun 1852.

96.   **George Washington Yoakum Sr.,** son of Valentine "Felty" Yoakum and Margaret See was
born on 16 Jan 1752 in Peach Creek, Virginia (Greenbrier County, WV (DAR Application)). He

died on 28 Oct 1800 in Cumberland Mountains, Grainger County, Tennessee (Killed by a bear while on a hunt in the Cumberland Mountains Buried at Rogers Cemetery in Speedwell, Claiborne Cty, TN). He married **Martha Van Bibber**, daughter of Rev. Isaac Michael Van Bibber Sr. and Sarah Davis in 1777 in Greenbrier, West Virginia.

97. **Martha Van Bibber**, daughter of Rev. Isaac Michael Van Bibber Sr. and Sarah Davis was born in 1754 in Greenbrier, Virginia. She died in 1829 in Salisbury, Sangamon County, Illinois.

Martha Van Bibber and George Washington Yoakum Sr. had the following children:

    i.   Isaac Yoakum, son of George Washington Yoakum Sr. and Martha Van Bibber was born on 23 Feb 1778 in Muddy Creek, Greenbrier County, Virginia. He died on 24 Jul 1857 in Powell Valley, Claiborne, Tennessee (Age at Death: 79). He married Mary Davis. She was born in 1779 in Claiborne County, Tennessee. She died in 1845 in Claiborne County, Tennessee.

    ii.   Peter Yoakum, son of George Washington Yoakum Sr. and Martha Van Bibber was born in 1781 in Muddy Creek, Greenbriar, Virginia. He died on 24 Jul 1857 in Vienna, Johnson, Illinois. He married Sarah Stinnet, daughter of Isham Stinnett IV and Elizabeth Austin in 1818 in Powell Valley, Claiborne, Tennessee. She was born on 14 Apr 1798 in Powell Valley, Claiborne, Tennessee. She died in 1860 in Pulaski, Pulaski, Illinois.

    iii.   John Yoakum, son of George Washington Yoakum Sr. and Martha Van Bibber was born on 07 Sep 1781 in Muddy Creek, Greenbriar, Virginia. He died on 09 Apr 1848 in Montgomery County, Illinois. He married Rachel Weaver. She was born in 1784 in Claiborne County, Tennessee. She died in 1866 in Montgomery County, Illinois.

    iv.   George Yoakum Jr, son of George Washington Yoakum Sr. and Martha Van Bibber was born on 30 Jul 1783 in Muddy Creek, Greenbrier County, Virginia. He died on 30 Mar 1841 in Madisonville, Monroe, Tennessee. He married Mary Ann Maddy on 27 May 1809. She was born on 25 Nov 1792 in Madisonville, Monroe, Tennessee, USA. She died on 27 Apr 1843 in Madisonville, Monroe, Tennessee, United States.

    v.   Valentine Yoakum, son of George Washington Yoakum Sr. and Martha Van Bibber was born in 1785 in Claiborne County, Tennessee. He died in 1830 in Roane, Tennessee. He married Charlotte Reynolds. She was born in 1788 in Claiborne, Tennessee. She died in 1830 in Roane, Tennessee.

48.   vi.   James Yoakum, son of George Washington Yoakum Sr. and Martha Van Bibber was born in 1787 in Greenbrier County, West Virginia. He died in 1834 in Menard County, Illinois. He married Julia Owens, daughter of William Owens and Elizabeth Meffin in 1810 in Claiborne County, Tennessee. She was born in 1787 in Claiborne, Tennessee. She died in 1832 in Menard County, Illinois.

    vii.   Jesse Yoakum, son of George Washington Yoakum Sr. and Martha Van Bibber was born in 1787 in Claiborne, Tennessee. He died in Taitsville, Ray, Missouri. He married Anna Berry. She was born in Powell Valley, Claiborne, Tennessee.

> viii. Robert Yoakum, son of George Washington Yoakum Sr. and Martha Van Bibber was born in 1789 in Lee, Virginia. He died on 29 Jan 1824 in Powell Valley, Claiborne, Tennessee. He married Parkey Berry.

> ix. William Yoakum, son of George Washington Yoakum Sr. and Martha Van Bibber was born on 27 Dec 1789 in Powell River, Russell, Virginia. He died on 17 Apr 1880 in Salisbury, Sangamon, Illinois (Age at Death: 90). He married Sarah Simmons on 03 May 1824 in Sangamon, Illinois. She was born on 25 Feb 1804 in Adair County, Kentucky. She died on 05 Dec 1865 in Salisbury, Sangamon, Illinois (Age: 61). He married Letitia (Rice) Henderson in Jan 1868 in Salisbury, Sangamon County, Illinois.

> x. Margaret Yoakum, daughter of George Washington Yoakum Sr. and Martha Van Bibber was born in 1790 in Greenbrier County, West Virginia. She died in 1824 in Claiborne, Tennessee. She married Dennis Condrey. He was born in Powell Valley, Claiborne, Tennessee.

> xi. Matthias Yoakum, son of George Washington Yoakum Sr. and Martha Van Bibber was born in 1800 in Claiborne County, Tennessee. He died on 27 Aug 1857 in Salisbury, Sangamon County, Illinois (Buried in Richland Baptist Church Cemetery). He married Elizabeth McHenry. She was born on 18 Feb 1800 in Virginia. She died on 11 May 1876 in Salisbury, Sangamon, Illinois.

98. **William Owens** was born in 1750 in Sussex County, Delaware. He died in 1815. He married **Elizabeth Meffin** on 28 Jan 1775 in Caroline County, Maryland.

99. **Elizabeth Meffin**.

Elizabeth Meffin and William Owens had the following child:

> 49. i. Julia Owens, daughter of William Owens and Elizabeth Meffin was born in 1787 in Claiborne, Tennessee. She died in 1832 in Menard County, Illinois. She married James Yoakum, son of George Washington Yoakum Sr. and Martha Van Bibber in 1810 in Claiborne County, Tennessee. He was born in 1787 in Greenbrier County, West Virginia. He died in 1834 in Menard County, Illinois.

100. **Rev. Robert Stewart Sr.**, son of Rev. William M. Stewart and Ann Park was born on 28 Dec 1762 in Clough, Antrim, Ireland. He died on 18 Mar 1846 in Greenville, Bond, Illinois.

101. **Margaret McCallen**, daughter of Robert McCallen and Mary Bradley was born in 1767 in Brownsville, Pennsylvania. She died on 19 May 1821 in Adams, Brown, Ohio.

Notes for Rev. Robert Stewart Sr.:
Robert Stewart Sr.
http://trees.ancestry.com/rd?f=image&guid=eacaccee-e8fa-4d23-8f7c-9c1d087c6a75&tid=251
61444&pid=201

Margaret McCallen and Rev. Robert Stewart Sr. had the following children:

        i.   Mary STEWART, daughter of Rev. Robert Stewart Sr. and Margaret McCallen was born in 1796 in Washington, Mason, Kentucky, USA. She died in 1834.

50.   ii.   Rev. William McCallen Stewart, son of Rev. Robert Stewart Sr. and Margaret McCallen was born on 24 Apr 1794 in On the Monongahela River, near Brownsville, Fayette, Pennsylvania (William was born on a flat boat as his parents Robert and Ann (Park) Stewart were emigrating to Kentucky. They landed in Kentucky at the place where Frankfort is now located. When they landed at the place of destination, William was only 6 days old.). He died on 12 Nov 1885 in Puyallup, Pierce, Washington. He married Ann Laughlin, daughter of John Laughlin Jr. and Mary Dalrymple on 22 Feb 1816 in Adams, Ohio. She was born on 21 May 1795 in Pendleton, Anderson, South Carolina. She died on 23 Mar 1847 in Cedar Rapids, Linn, Iowa (Buried in Brockman Cemetery, Cedar Rapids, Linn County, Iowa). He married Phoebe ROSS on 17 Aug 1847 in Linn, Iowa. She was born on 04 Jul 1817 in Mercer, Pennsylvania, USA. She died on 20 Jul 1848 in Marion, Iowa, USA. He married Mary Cochran ROBB on 20 Nov 1850 in Marion, Linn, Iowa. She was born on 13 Aug 1816 in Mercer, Pennsylvania, USA. She died on 26 Jan 1873 in Carbondale, Jackson, Illinois, USA.

        iii.   Rev. Robert R Stewart Jr., son of Rev. Robert Stewart Sr. and Margaret McCallen was born on 03 May 1798 in Maysville, Mason, Kentucky, USA. He died on 11 Jul 1881 in Troy, Madison, Illinois, USA.

        iv.   Ann Stewart, daughter of Rev. Robert Stewart Sr. and Margaret McCallen was born on 19 Jul 1800 in Washington, Mason, Kentucky. She died on 10 Oct 1885 in La Grande, Union, Oregon.

        v.   John R STEWART, son of Rev. Robert Stewart Sr. and Margaret McCallen was born in 1801 in Eagle Creek, Adams, Ohio, USA. He died in 1834 in Brown, Ohio, United States.

        vi.   Margaret R STEWART, daughter of Rev. Robert Stewart Sr. and Margaret McCallen was born in 1803 in Eagle Creek, Adams, Ohio, USA. She died in 1803 in Eagle Creek, Adams, Ohio, USA.

        vii.   Sarah R STEWART, daughter of Rev. Robert Stewart Sr. and Margaret McCallen was born on 09 Jun 1805 in Eagle Creek, Adams, Ohio, USA. She died in United States.

        viii.   Elizabeth R STEWART, daughter of Rev. Robert Stewart Sr. and Margaret McCallen was born in 1808 in Eagle Creek, Adams, Ohio, USA.

        ix.   James Park STUART, son of Rev. Robert Stewart Sr. and Margaret McCallen was born on 29 Jan 1810 in Eagle Creek, Adams, Ohio, USA. He died on 29 Jun 1882 in Sommerset, Pennsylvania, United States.

102.   **John Laughlin Jr.,** son of John Luke Laughlin Sr. and Mary White was born on 16 Sep 1769 in

Big Spring, Cumberland, Pennsylvania. He died on 27 Sep 1852 in Shoal Creek, Bond, Illinois. He married **Mary Dalrymple,** daughter of Samuel Dalrymple and Sarah Pollock on 16 Jun 1794 in Pendleton, South Carolina.

103.   **Mary Dalrymple**, daughter of Samuel Dalrymple and Sarah Pollock was born on 16 Jun 1776 in Pendleton, Anderson, South Carolina. She died on 16 Jun 1867 in Union Grove, Putnam, Illinois.

Mary Dalrymple and John Laughlin Jr. had the following children:

     i.   Samuel Davis Laughlin, son of John Laughlin Jr. and Mary Dalrymple was born on 26 Feb 1797 in Pendleton Co., SC. He died on 15 Feb 1849 in Union Grove, Putnam Co., IL.

     ii.   John Newton Laughlin, son of John Laughlin Jr. and Mary Dalrymple was born on 13 Mar 1799 in Pendleton Co., SC. He died in 1852.

     iii.   Elizabeth Laughlin, daughter of John Laughlin Jr. and Mary Dalrymple was born on 15 Jun 1801 in Pendleton Co., SC. She died in 1856.

51.   iv.   Ann Laughlin, daughter of John Laughlin Jr. and Mary Dalrymple was born on 21 May 1795 in Pendleton, Anderson, South Carolina. She died on 23 Mar 1847 in Cedar Rapids, Linn, Iowa (Buried in Brockman Cemetery, Cedar Rapids, Linn County, Iowa). She married Rev. William McCallen Stewart, son of Rev. Robert Stewart Sr. and Margaret McCallen on 22 Feb 1816 in Adams, Ohio. He was born on 24 Apr 1794 in On the Monongahela River, near Brownsville, Fayette, Pennsylvania (William was born on a flat boat as his parents Robert and Ann (Park) Stewart were emigrating to Kentucky. They landed in Kentucky at the place where Frankfort is now located. When they landed at the place of destination, William was only 6 days old.). He died on 12 Nov 1885 in Puyallup, Pierce, Washington.

     v.   Sarah Laughlin, daughter of John Laughlin Jr. and Mary Dalrymple was born on 11 Aug 1803 in Pendleton Co., SC.

     vi.   James Gilliland Laughlin, son of John Laughlin Jr. and Mary Dalrymple was born on 13 Nov 1805 in Pendleton Co., SC. He died in 1895.

     vii.   Mary Laughlin, daughter of John Laughlin Jr. and Mary Dalrymple was born on 13 Sep 1806 in Red Oak, Brown Co., OH. She died in 1881.

     viii.   Nancy Laughlin, daughter of John Laughlin Jr. and Mary Dalrymple was born on 17 Dec 1810 in Red Oak, Brown Co., OH. She died on 28 Sep 1887.

     ix.   Thomas Williamson Laughlin, son of John Laughlin Jr. and Mary Dalrymple was born on 17 Dec 1813 in Red Oak, Brown Co., OH. He died in 1860.

     x.   Alexander Martin Laughlin, son of John Laughlin Jr. and Mary Dalrymple was born on 18 May 1816 in Red Oak, Brown Co., OH. He died on 17 Nov 1897.

xi. Rosanna Laughlin, daughter of John Laughlin Jr. and Mary Dalrymple was born on 30 Jan 1820 in Shoal Creek, Bond Co., IL.

xii. Mary Laughlin, daughter of John Laughlin Jr. and Mary Dalrymple was born on 13 Sep 1808 in Brown, Ohio, United States. She died on 28 Sep 1887 in Illinois, United States.

104. **James Duncan**, son of Marshall Duncan and Mary Ann Durron was born in 1755 in Rowan, Surry, North Carolina (Stokes county was formed in 1789 from Surry Co.). He died in 1840 in Salisbury, Sangamon, Illinois. He married **Averilla "Ava" Shelton**, daughter of John Shelton and Elizabeth Lawson in 1774 in North Carolina.

105. **Averilla "Ava" Shelton**, daughter of John Shelton and Elizabeth Lawson was born in 1755 in Surry, North Carolina. She died in 1834 in Salisbury, Sangamon, Illinois.

Averilla "Ava" Shelton and James Duncan had the following children:

52. i. Marshall Duncan, son of James Duncan and Averilla "Ava" Shelton was born in 1783 in Stokes, North Carolina. He died on 03 Dec 1858 in Salisbury, Sangamon, Illinois. He married Hannah Miller. She was born about 1790 in Kentucky, USA. She died in USA. He married Rachel Thrasher. She was born on 03 Aug 1785 in Kentucky.

ii. George Duncan, son of James Duncan and Averilla "Ava" Shelton was born in 1805 in Adair, Kentucky, USA.

iii. Susannah Duncan, daughter of James Duncan and Averilla "Ava" Shelton was born in 1802 in Stokes, North Carolina. She died in 1827 in Russell, Kentucky.

iv. William Duncan, son of James Duncan and Averilla "Ava" Shelton was born in 1807 in Kentucky.

v. Avarilla Duncan, daughter of James Duncan and Averilla "Ava" Shelton was born in 1796 in Stokes, North Carolina. She died in 1854 in Morgan, Illinois.

vi. Cynthia Duncan, daughter of James Duncan and Averilla "Ava" Shelton was born on 24 Jun 1800 in Stokes, North Carolina. She died on 19 May 1889 in Sangamon County.

vii. James Duncan, son of James Duncan and Averilla "Ava" Shelton was born in 1792 in Stokes, North Carolina. He died in 1869 in Russell, Kentucky.

viii. Sarah Duncan, daughter of James Duncan and Averilla "Ava" Shelton was born in 1784 in Stokes, North Carolina. She died in Clark, Kentucky.

ix. John Sr Duncan, son of James Duncan and Averilla "Ava" Shelton was born in 1787 in Stokes, North Carolina, USA. He died in 1863 in Salisbury, Sangamon, Illinois, USA.

x. Jane Duncan, daughter of James Duncan and Averilla "Ava" Shelton was born in 1772 in Willistown, Chester, Pennsylvania. She died on 29 Nov 1846 in Moniteau, Missouri.

xi. Rice Duncan, son of James Duncan and Averilla "Ava" Shelton was born on 05 Mar 1781 in Stokes, North Carolina. He died on 07 Oct 1863 in Salisbury, Sangamon, Illinois. He married Barbara Antle, daughter of Henry Antle Sr. and Mary "Polly" Abrell on 15 Mar 1806 in Adair County, Kentucky. She was born in 1785 in Frederick, Virginia. She died in 1812 in Kentucky.

xii. Mary Polly Duncan, daughter of James Duncan and Averilla "Ava" Shelton was born in 1764 in Stokes, North Carolina, USA. She died in 1830.

xiii. Charles Duncan, son of James Duncan and Averilla "Ava" Shelton was born in 1807 in Kentucky. He died on 06 Apr 1893 in Miller, Missouri.

xiv. George Duncan, son of James Duncan and Averilla "Ava" Shelton was born in 1801. He died on 09 Jun 1875 in Russell, Kentucky.

xv. Mary Polly Duncan, daughter of James Duncan and Averilla "Ava" Shelton was born in 1780. She died in 1816 in Clay, Missouri.

106. **William Thrasher** was born in 1745 in England. He died in Mar 1796 in Burke County, North Carolina. He married **Sarah Elizabeth Phillips**.

107. **Sarah Elizabeth Phillips** was born on 24 Aug 1755 in Westerleigh, Gloucestershire, England. She died in 1805 in Burke, North Carolina.

Sarah Elizabeth Phillips and William Thrasher had the following child:

53. i. Rachel Thrasher, daughter of William Thrasher and Sarah Elizabeth Phillips was born on 03 Aug 1785 in Kentucky. She married Marshall Duncan. He was born in 1783 in Stokes, North Carolina. He died on 03 Dec 1858 in Salisbury, Sangamon, Illinois.

108. **George Miller** was born in 1747 in Darmstadt, Hesse, Germany. He died in 1804 in Crocus, Adair, Kentucky. He married **Elizabeth Beaxton**.

109. **Elizabeth Beaxton** was born in 1752 in Port Royal, Caroline, Virginia. She died in 1832 in Crocus, Adair, Kentucky.

Elizabeth Beaxton and George Miller had the following children:

i. George Miller, son of George Miller and Elizabeth Beaxton was born in 1796 in Green, Kentucky, United States. He died in 1880 in Lincoln, Logan, Illinois, United States.

ii. Mathias Miller, son of George Miller and Elizabeth Beaxton was born in 1793 in Kentucky, United States. He died in 1794.

54. iii. Solomon Miller, son of George Miller and Elizabeth Beaxton was born on 11 May

1796 in Adair, Kentucky. He died on 07 Jun 1857 in Salisbury, Sangamon, Illinois. He married Nancy Ann Antle, daughter of Henry Antle Sr. and Mary "Polly" Abrell on 13 Aug 1813 in Adair County, Kentucky. She was born on 26 Dec 1792 in Lincoln, Kentucky. She died on 01 Apr 1854 in Salisbury, Sangamon, Illinois.

   iv.   David Miller, son of George Miller and Elizabeth Beaxton was born on 15 Aug 1790 in Lincoln, Loudoun, Virginia, United States. He died on 10 Nov 1868 in Vermont, Fulton, Illinois, United States.

   v.   Aaron Miller, son of George Miller and Elizabeth Beaxton was born on 09 Jan 1786 in Lincoln, Loudoun, Virginia, United States. He died on 15 Mar 1866 in Jackson, Keokuk, Iowa, United States.

   vi.   Adam Miller, son of George Miller and Elizabeth Beaxton was born in 1784 in Lincoln, Loudoun, Virginia, United States. He died on 03 Feb 1849 in Crocus, Adair, Kentucky, United States.

   vii.   Henry Miller, son of George Miller and Elizabeth Beaxton was born in 1780 in Kentucky, Virginia, United States. He died in 1810 in Sangamon County, Illinois, USA.

   viii.   Christopher Miller, son of George Miller and Elizabeth Beaxton was born in 1778 in Kentucky, Virginia, United States. He died on 23 Jan 1816 in Cumberland, Kentucky, United States.

   ix.   Moses Miller, son of George Miller and Elizabeth Beaxton was born in 1777 in Crocus, Kentucky, United States. He died in 1814 in Sangamon County, Illinois, USA.

   x.   Jacob Miller, son of George Miller and Elizabeth Beaxton was born on 08 Apr 1775 in Fincastle, Botetourt, Virginia. He died in 1852 in Sangamon, Illinois.

110.   **Henry Antle Sr.**, son of Peter Antle and Ann ?? was born in 1753 in Bullskin Run, Frederick, Virginia. He died in 1805 in Cumberland, Kentucky. He married **Mary "Polly" Abrell**, daughter of John Abrell and Anna Maria Lang in 1771 in Winchester, Frederick, Virginia.

111.   **Mary "Polly" Abrell**, daughter of John Abrell and Anna Maria Lang was born in 1752 in Green, Forest, Pennsylvania. She died on 15 Aug 1823 in Sangamon, Illinois.

Mary "Polly" Abrell and Henry Antle Sr. had the following children:

   i.   Katherine Antle Davis, daughter of Henry Antle Sr. and Mary "Polly" Abrell was born in 1783 in Berkeley, WV, USA. She died in 1846 in Salisbury, Sangamon, Illinois, United States.

   ii.   Rev. John Antle, son of Henry Antle Sr. and Mary "Polly" Abrell was born on 15 Apr 1789 in Lincoln, Kentucky. He died on 30 Aug 1864 in Salisbury, Sangamon, Illinois.

iii.   Martha "Patsy" Antle, daughter of Henry Antle Sr. and Mary "Polly" Abrell was born in 1790 in Frederick, Virginia, United States. She died in Aug 1823 in Cass County, Illinois, USA.

iv.   Malinda Almira Antle, daughter of Henry Antle Sr. and Mary "Polly" Abrell was born in 1813 in Kentucky, United States. She died on 06 May 1892 in Barry, Missouri, United States.

55.   v.   Nancy Ann Antle, daughter of Henry Antle Sr. and Mary "Polly" Abrell was born on 26 Dec 1792 in Lincoln, Kentucky. She died on 01 Apr 1854 in Salisbury, Sangamon, Illinois. She married Solomon Miller, son of George Miller and Elizabeth Beaxton on 13 Aug 1813 in Adair County, Kentucky. He was born on 11 May 1796 in Adair, Kentucky. He died on 07 Jun 1857 in Salisbury, Sangamon, Illinois. She married ?? Duncan in 1811 in Kentucky.

vi.   Ceny Antle, son of Henry Antle Sr. and Mary "Polly" Abrell was born in 1788. He died on 02 Jul 1859.

vii.   Henry Antle Jr., son of Henry Antle Sr. and Mary "Polly" Abrell was born on 23 Dec 1779 in Frederick, Virginia. He died on 02 Jul 1859 in Dry Fork, Kentucky. He married Mary "Polly" Simmons. She was born in 1780 in Tennessee. She died on 03 Feb 1806 in Adair County, Kentucky.

viii.   Mary "Polly" Antle, daughter of Henry Antle Sr. and Mary "Polly" Abrell was born in 1780 in Frederick, Virginia, United States. She died in 1853 in Sangamon, Illinois, United States.

ix.   Elizabeth Antle, daughter of Henry Antle Sr. and Mary "Polly" Abrell was born in 1781 in Frederick, Virginia, United States. She died in 1870 in Sangamon, Illinois, United States. She married John Antle Miller. He was born on 08 Apr 1822 in Salisbury, Sangamon County, Illinois. He died on 02 Nov 1899 in Salisbury, Sangamon County, Illinois.

x.   Jacob Millwright Antle Sr., son of Henry Antle Sr. and Mary "Polly" Abrell was born in 1782 in Frederick County, Winchester, VA. He died on 27 Feb 1858 in Russell, Russell, Kentucky, USA.

xi.   Michael Antle, son of Henry Antle Sr. and Mary "Polly" Abrell was born on 09 Dec 1784 in Frederick, Virginia, United States. He died on 08 Sep 1853 in Morgan, Illinois, United States.

xii.   Barbara Antle, daughter of Henry Antle Sr. and Mary "Polly" Abrell was born in 1785 in Frederick, Virginia. She died in 1812 in Kentucky. She married Rice Duncan, son of James Duncan and Averilla "Ava" Shelton on 15 Mar 1806 in Adair County, Kentucky. He was born on 05 Mar 1781 in Stokes, North Carolina. He died on 07 Oct 1863 in Salisbury, Sangamon, Illinois.

112.   Roderick MacDonald was born in Scotland. He died in 1842. He married **? Christian**.

113.   **? Christian**.

? Christian and Roderick MacDonald had the following children:

56.   i.   Hugh MacDonald, son of Roderick MacDonald and ? Christian was born in 1795 in
                Scotland. He died on 06 Oct 1860 in Wallace Harbor, Nova Scotia, Canada (He
                apparantly drowned in Wallace Harbour (Cumberland County) while attempting
                to board a schooner. A short newspaper article about the incident (dated
                November 3, 1860) states that the body had yet to be recovered, and that
                anyone finding it will "confer a). He married Mary ?.

         ii.   Margaret MacDonald.

         iii.   Duncan MacDonald, son of Roderick MacDonald and ? Christian was born in 1810
                in Pictou, Nova Scotia, Canada. He died on 18 Apr 1869. He married Eleanor
                Dewar.

         iv.   Ann MacDonald, daughter of Roderick MacDonald and ? Christian was born in
                1810.

Generation 8

140.   **Christian Lenhart**, son of Johan Peter Lenhart and Maria Margaretha was born in 1722 in
        Germany. He died on 15 Apr 1810 in Wilkens Twp, Allegheny, Pennsylvania. He married **Anna
        Maria Heindler**, daughter of Johan Adam Heindler on 05 Jun 1764 in York, Pennsylvania.

141.   **Anna Maria Heindler**, daughter of Johan Adam Heindler was born in 1740 in Germany. She
        died on 09 Feb 1827 in Wilkins, Allegheny, Pennsylvania.

Anna Maria Heindler and Christian Lenhart had the following children:

         i.   Jacob Linhart, son of Christian Lenhart and Anna Maria Heindler was born on 24
                Oct 1773 in York, York, Pennsylvania, United States. He died on 14 Dec 1844 in
                Pittsburgh, Allegheny, Pennsylvania, United States.

         ii.   Christian Linhart, son of Christian Lenhart and Anna Maria Heindler was born on
                24 Jul 1771 in York, York, Pennsylvania, United States. He died on 08 Sep 1844 in
                North Huntington, Westmoreland, Pennsylvania, United States.

         iii.   Michael Linhart, son of Christian Lenhart and Anna Maria Heindler was born on
                10 Jan 1770 in York, York, Pennsylvania, United States. He died on 31 Oct 1818 in
                Wilkins, Allegheny, Pennsylvania, United States.

         iv.   Barbara Linhart, daughter of Christian Lenhart and Anna Maria Heindler was
                born on 20 Mar 1768 in York, York, Pennsylvania, United States.

         v.   Hannah Linhart, daughter of Christian Lenhart and Anna Maria Heindler was
                born on 09 Feb 1784.

         vi.   Abraham Linhart, son of Christian Lenhart and Anna Maria Heindler was born on
                11 Mar 1782 in Allegheny, Pennsylvania, United States. He died on 22 Feb 1838 in

Westmoreland, Pennsylvania, United States.

vii. Elizabeth Linhart, daughter of Christian Lenhart and Anna Maria Heindler was born in 1779 in York, York, Pennsylvania, United States.

viii. Dorothy Linhart, daughter of Christian Lenhart and Anna Maria Heindler was born in 1775 in York, York, Pennsylvania, United States. She died in Feb 1804.

ix. Samuel Linhart, son of Christian Lenhart and Anna Maria Heindler was born in 1782 in York, York, Pennsylvania, United States. He died on 28 May 1831.

x. Margaretha Mary Linhart, daughter of Christian Lenhart and Anna Maria Heindler was born on 06 Dec 1780 in York, York, Pennsylvania, United States. She died on 28 Jun 1861 in Wilkins, Allegheny, Pennsylvania, United States.

70. xi. John Adam Linhart, son of Christian Lenhart and Anna Maria Heindler was born in 1765 in York, York, Pennsylvania. He died on 05 Jul 1848 in Wilkins, Alleghany, Pennsylvania. He married Maria Sara Baughman, daughter of Heinrich Baughman Jr. and Anna Catherina Kunkle in 1794 in Pitt, Allegheny, Pennsylvania. She was born on 06 Jun 1771 in Upper Hanover, Montgomery, Pennsylvania. She died in 1827 in Wilkins, Alleghany, Pennsylvania.

142. **Heinrich Baughman Jr.**, son of Heinrich Baughman and Anne was born in 1742 in Hamburg, Germany. He died on 18 May 1814 in North Huntingdon, Westmoreland, Pennsylvania, United States. He married **Anna Catherina Kunkle**, daughter of Johannes Kunkle and Anna Magdalena Kaiser in 1764 in Montgomery, Pennsylvania.

143. **Anna Catherina Kunkle**, daughter of Johannes Kunkle and Anna Magdalena Kaiser was born on 25 Sep 1745 in Fleorsbach, Geinhausen, Hessen, Germany. She died on 10 May 1814 in Irwin, Westmoreland, Pennsylvania.

Anna Catherina Kunkle and Heinrich Baughman Jr. had the following children:

i. Johanne (John) Baughman, son of Heinrich Baughman Jr. and Anna Catherina Kunkle was born on 16 Apr 1767 in Upper Hanover, Montgomery, Pennsylvania, USA. He died in 1831 in N Huntingdon, Westmoreland, Pennsylvania, United States.

ii. Margaretha Elisabetha Bachman, daughter of Heinrich Baughman Jr. and Anna Catherina Kunkle was born on 05 Aug 1765 in Upper Hanover, Montgomery, Pennsylvania.

iii. Barbara Baughman, daughter of Heinrich Baughman Jr. and Anna Catherina Kunkle was born on 06 Jun 1768 in Upper Hanover, Montgomery, Pennsylvania. She died on 22 Sep 1839 in Westmoreland, Pennsylvania, USA.

71. iv. Maria Sara Baughman, daughter of Heinrich Baughman Jr. and Anna Catherina Kunkle was born on 06 Jun 1771 in Upper Hanover, Montgomery, Pennsylvania. She died in 1827 in Wilkins, Alleghany, Pennsylvania. She married John Adam

Linhart, son of Christian Lenhart and Anna Maria Heindler in 1794 in Pitt, Allegheny, Pennsylvania. He was born in 1765 in York, York, Pennsylvania. He died on 05 Jul 1848 in Wilkins, Alleghany, Pennsylvania.

v.   Anna Catherina Bachman, daughter of Heinrich Baughman Jr. and Anna Catherina Kunkle was born on 25 Dec 1769 in Upper Hanover Twp., Montgomery Co., Pa.. She died on 21 Sep 1857 in Butler, Butler, Pennsylvania, United States.

vi.   George Heinrich Bachman, son of Heinrich Baughman Jr. and Anna Catherina Kunkle was born on 02 Feb 1773 in Upper Hanover Twp., Montgomery Co., Pa.. He died on 16 Dec 1775 in Upper Hanover Twp., Montgomery Co., Pa..

vii.   Johannes Heinrich Bachman, son of Heinrich Baughman Jr. and Anna Catherina Kunkle was born on 09 May 1780 in Upper Hanover Twp., Montgomery Co., Pa.. He died on 25 Jun 1803 in North Huntingdon Twp. Westmoreland Co. Pa..

viii.   John Adam Baughman, son of Heinrich Baughman Jr. and Anna Catherina Kunkle was born on 02 Feb 1773 in Upper Hanover, Montgomery, Pennsylvania. He died on 23 Jul 1840 in Westmoreland, Pennsylvania, USA.

ix.   Peter Baughman, son of Heinrich Baughman Jr. and Anna Catherina Kunkle was born on 23 Jan 1778 in Upper Hanover, Montgomery, Pennsylavania. He died on 23 May 1830 in Westmoreland, Westmoreland, Pennsylvania, USA.

192.   **Valentine "Felty" Yoakum**, son of Mathias Joachim and Maria Barbara Uhngefehr was born on 08 Sep 1722 in Edigheim, Bayern, Germany. He died on 17 Jul 1763 in Muddy Creek Massacre, Greenbrier, Virginia. He married **Margaret See**, daughter of Johann George Zeh Jr. and Mary Margaret Tschudi in 1748 in Hardy, West Virginia.

193.   **Margaret See**, daughter of Johann George Zeh Jr. and Mary Margaret Tschudi was born in 1725 in Mohawk, Schoharie, New York. She died on 11 Mar 1815 in Franklin, Coshocton, Ohio.

Notes for Margaret See:
Indian Captives
http://trees.ancestry.com/rd?f=document&guid=c2589143-eed2-4fce-82e5-d0bd713cc917&tid=25161444&pid=159

Margaret See and Valentine "Felty" Yoakum had the following children:
i.   Elizabeth Yoakum, daughter of Valentine "Felty" Yoakum and Margaret See was born in 1751 in Hardy, Bedford, Virginia. She died on 04 Dec 1839 in Millerstown, Perry, Pennsylvania. She married John Shoemaker on 13 Aug 1782 in Greenbrier County, West Virginia.

96.   ii.   George Washington Yoakum Sr., son of Valentine "Felty" Yoakum and Margaret See was born on 16 Jan 1752 in Peach Creek, Virginia (Greenbrier County, WV (DAR Application)). He died on 28 Oct 1800 in Cumberland Mountains, Grainger County, Tennessee (Killed by a bear while on a hunt in the Cumberland

Mountains Buried at Rogers Cemetery in Speedwell, Claiborne Cty, TN). He married Martha Van Bibber, daughter of Rev. Isaac Michael Van Bibber Sr. and Sarah Davis in 1777 in Greenbrier, West Virginia. She was born in 1754 in Greenbrier, Virginia. She died in 1829 in Salisbury, Sangamon County, Illinois.

    iii.   John Yoakum, son of Valentine "Felty" Yoakum and Margaret See was born in 1755 in Greenbrier, Virginia. He died in 1791 in Claiborne, Tennessee.

    iv.   Sarah Yoakum, daughter of Valentine "Felty" Yoakum and Margaret See was born in 1758 in Greenbrier, West Virginia. She died on 08 Oct 1838. She married Peter Van Bibber III. He was born on 15 Aug 1757 in Halifax, Virginia.

194.   **Rev. Isaac Michael Van Bibber Sr.**, son of Peter Van Bibber Sr. and Ann Honriette Gooding was born on 02 Feb 1724 in Strasburg, Chester, Pennsylvania. He died on 10 Oct 1774 in Battle of Point Pleasant, Mason, West Virginia (died in battle). He married **Sarah Davis** in 1750 in North Carolina.

195.   **Sarah Davis** was born in 1725 in Strasburg, Chester, Pennsylvania. She died on 05 Jan 1800 in Greenbrier, Virginia.

Sarah Davis and Rev. Isaac Michael Van Bibber Sr. had the following children:

    i.   Rebecca Van Bibber, daughter of Rev. Isaac Michael Van Bibber Sr. and Sarah Davis was born in 1769.

    ii.   Isaac Van Bibber Jr., son of Rev. Isaac Michael Van Bibber Sr. and Sarah Davis was born on 12 Oct 1771 in Greenbrier County, West Virginia. He died on 30 Sep 1840 in Williamsburg, Callaway, Missouri.

    iii.   John Van Bibber, son of Rev. Isaac Michael Van Bibber Sr. and Sarah Davis was born in 1765 in Russell, Virginia. He died on 15 Nov 1822 in Claiborne, Tennessee. He married Margaret Crisman, daughter of Isaac Crisman and Jean Scott in 1787.

    iv.   James Van Bibber, son of Rev. Isaac Michael Van Bibber Sr. and Sarah Davis was born on 08 May 1766 in Halifax, Virginia. He died on 19 Dec 1834 in Claiborne, Tennessee. He married Hannah Hoover.

    v.   Peter Van Bibber, son of Rev. Isaac Michael Van Bibber Sr. and Sarah Davis was born on 05 Aug 1757 in Lunenberg, Virginia. He died on 08 Oct 1838 in Greenbriar, West Virginia. He married Eleanor Van Bibber, daughter of Peter Van Bibber Jr. and Margary Bounds on 29 Jun 1785 in Greenbrier, Virginia. She was born in 1762 in Halifax, Virginia. She died in 1840 in Clairborne, Tennessee.

    vi.   Matthew Van Bibber, son of Rev. Isaac Michael Van Bibber Sr. and Sarah Davis was born in 1770.

    vii.   Nancy Van Bibber, daughter of Rev. Isaac Michael Van Bibber Sr. and Sarah Davis was born in 1759 in Virginia. She died on 27 Dec 1866 in Van Buren, Tennessee. She married Robert Howard. He was born in 1762 in Greenbrier, Virginia. He died on 09 Oct 1832 in White, Tennessee.

97.   viii.   Martha Van Bibber, daughter of Rev. Isaac Michael Van Bibber Sr. and Sarah
                Davis was born in 1754 in Greenbrier, Virginia. She died in 1829 in Salisbury,
                Sangamon County, Illinois. She married George Washington Yoakum Sr., son of
                Valentine "Felty" Yoakum and Margaret See in 1777 in Greenbrier, West Virginia.
                He was born on 16 Jan 1752 in Peach Creek, Virginia (Greenbrier County, WV
                (DAR Application)). He died on 28 Oct 1800 in Cumberland Mountains, Grainger
                County, Tennessee (Killed by a bear while on a hunt in the Cumberland
                Mountains Buried at Rogers Cemetery in Speedwell, Claiborne Cty, TN).

200.   **Rev. William M. Stewart**, son of Robert Thomas Stewart and Rachel Maxwell was born in 1722
       in Clough, Antrim, Ireland. He died in 1804 in Adams, Brown, Ohio. He married **Ann Park** on 07
       Jul 1762 in Clough, Antrim, Ireland.

201.   **Ann Park** was born in 1725 in Clough, Antrim, Ireland. She died in 1787 in Cumberland Valle,
       Fayette, Pennsylvania.

       Ann Park and Rev. William M. Stewart had the following children:

       100.   i.   Rev. Robert Stewart Sr., son of Rev. William M. Stewart and Ann Park was born
                       on 28 Dec 1762 in Clough, Antrim, Ireland. He died on 18 Mar 1846 in Greenville,
                       Bond, Illinois. She was born in 1767 in Brownsville, Pennsylvania. She died on 19
                       May 1821 in Adams, Brown, Ohio.

               ii.   Margaret Stewart, daughter of Rev. William M. Stewart and Ann Park was born
                       on 10 Oct 1761 in Clough, Antrim, Ireland. She died on 10 Oct 1861 in Tyrone,
                       Fayette, Pennsylvania, United States.

               iii.   Ann Stewart, daughter of Rev. William M. Stewart and Ann Park was born on 05
                       Aug 1765 in Atlantic, Ocean, New Jersey, United States. She died on 01 Oct 1823
                       in Elizaville, Fleming, Kentucky, United States.

               iv.   Mary Stewart, daughter of Rev. William M. Stewart and Ann Park was born in
                       1767 in Fayette City, Fayette, Pennsylvania, United States.

               v.   James Stewart, son of Rev. William M. Stewart and Ann Park was born on 28
                       May 1755 in Clough, Antrim, Ireland. He died on 15 Sep 1833 in Mt Vernon, Linn,
                       Iowa, United States.

202.   **Robert McCallen** was born on 01 May 1749 in Pennsylvania. He died on 25 Dec 1821 in
       Harrison, Harrison, Indiana.

203.   **Mary Bradley**, daughter of Daniel Bradley and Margaret was born on 14 Oct 1752 in
       Connecticut. She died on 12 Oct 1821 in Palmyra, Washington, Indiana.

       Mary Bradley and Robert McCallen had the following children:

               i.   Hays McCallen, son of Robert McCallen and Mary Bradley was born on 01 Jan
                       1777 in Berkeley, James, Virginia, USA.

101.   ii.   Margaret McCallen, daughter of Robert McCallen and Mary Bradley was born in 1767 in Brownsville, Pennsylvania. She died on 19 May 1821 in Adams, Brown, Ohio. He was born on 28 Dec 1762 in Clough, Antrim, Ireland. He died on 18 Mar 1846 in Greenville, Bond, Illinois.

       iii.   Mary McCallen, daughter of Robert McCallen and Mary Bradley was born on 18 Aug 1772 in Lancaster, Lancaster, Pennsylvania, USA.

       iv.   Sarah McAllen, daughter of Robert McCallen and Mary Bradley was born on 28 Mar 1774 in Pennsylvania, United States. She died on 15 Oct 1857 in Fleming, Kentucky, United States.

       v.   Isabelle McCallen, daughter of Robert McCallen and Mary Bradley was born in 1767.

204.   **John Luke Laughlin Sr.**, son of William Laughlin and Nancy Hodges was born in 1734 in Antrim, Northern Ireland. He died in 1774 in Pendleton District, South Carolina. He married **Mary White**, daughter of Anthony White and Mary Ralston in 1759 in Philadelphia, Pennsylvania.

205.   **Mary White**, daughter of Anthony White and Mary Ralston was born in 1745 in Quenbey, Scotland. She died in 1773 in Caldwell County, Kentucky.

Mary White and John Luke Laughlin Sr. had the following children:
       i.   Sarah Laughlin, daughter of John Luke Laughlin Sr. and Mary White was born in 1758 in Cumberland, Pennsylvania, United States. She died in Apr 1825 in Bond, Illinois, United States.

       ii.   Polly Laughlin, daughter of John Luke Laughlin Sr. and Mary White was born in 1757 in Cumberland, Pennsylvania, United States. She died in 1761.

       iii.   Anthony W Laughlin, son of John Luke Laughlin Sr. and Mary White was born on 07 Oct 1756 in Big Spring, Cumberland, Pennsylvania, United States. He died on 18 May 1837 in Caldwell, Kentucky, United States.

102.   iv.   John Laughlin Jr., son of John Luke Laughlin Sr. and Mary White was born on 16 Sep 1769 in Big Spring, Cumberland, Pennsylvania. He died on 27 Sep 1852 in Shoal Creek, Bond, Illinois. He married Mary Dalrymple, daughter of Samuel Dalrymple and Sarah Pollock on 16 Jun 1794 in Pendleton, South Carolina. She was born on 16 Jun 1776 in Pendleton, Anderson, South Carolina. She died on 16 Jun 1867 in Union Grove, Putnam, Illinois.

       v.   James Laughlin, son of John Luke Laughlin Sr. and Mary White was born in 1765 in Big Springs, Cumberland, Pennsylvania, United States. He died in Aug 1816 in McMinnville, Yamhill, Oregon, United States.

       vi.   Nancy Laughlin, daughter of John Luke Laughlin Sr. and Mary White was born in 1763 in Big Spring, Cumberland, Pennsylvania, United States. She died in 1777.

vii. Mary Laughlin, daughter of John Luke Laughlin Sr. and Mary White was born in 1760 in Cumberland, Pennsylvania, United States. She died on 15 Dec 1846 in Caldwell, Kentucky, United States.

206. **Samuel Dalrymple**, son of George Dalrymple and Rose Mason was born in 1755 in Newberry, Newberry, South Carolina. He died in 1791 in Abbeville, Abbeville, South Carolina (Buried at Abbeville, Anderson, SC). He married **Sarah Pollock**, daughter of James Pollock and Ann Wilson in 1771 in Laurens, Laurens, South Carolina.

207. **Sarah Pollock**, daughter of James Pollock and Ann Wilson was born in 1755 in Pendleton, Anderson, South Carolina. She died in Feb 1837 in Pendleton, Anderson, South Carolina.

Sarah Pollock and Samuel Dalrymple had the following children:

103.   i. Mary Dalrymple, daughter of Samuel Dalrymple and Sarah Pollock was born on 16 Jun 1776 in Pendleton, Anderson, South Carolina. She died on 16 Jun 1867 in Union Grove, Putnam, Illinois. She married John Laughlin Jr., son of John Luke Laughlin Sr. and Mary White on 16 Jun 1794 in Pendleton, South Carolina. He was born on 16 Sep 1769 in Big Spring, Cumberland, Pennsylvania. He died on 27 Sep 1852 in Shoal Creek, Bond, Illinois.

ii. Elizabeth Dalrymple, daughter of Samuel Dalrymple and Sarah Pollock was born in 1785 in Carolina, Carolina, Puerto Rico, United States. She died in 1874 in Carrol, Georgia, United States.

iii. Rachel Dalrymple, daughter of Samuel Dalrymple and Sarah Pollock was born in 1769. She died in 1785.

iv. Rebeckah, daughter of Samuel Dalrymple and Sarah Pollock was born in 1769. She died in 1774.

v. Rossanah Dalrymple, daughter of Samuel Dalrymple and Sarah Pollock was born in 1769. She died in 1785.

vi. Ann G Dalrymple, daughter of Samuel Dalrymple and Sarah Pollock was born on 22 Dec 1784 in Pendleton, Anderson, South Carolina, United States. She died in 1874 in Carrollton, Carroll, Georgia, United States.

vii. James Dalrymple, son of Samuel Dalrymple and Sarah Pollock was born in 1782 in Pendleton, Anderson, South Carolina, United States. He died in 1860 in Anderson, South Carolina, United States.

viii. Sarah DALRYMPLE, daughter of Samuel Dalrymple and Sarah Pollock was born in 1773 in Pendleton, Kentucky, United States. She died in 1847 in Linn, Osage, Missouri, United States.

208. **Marshall Duncan**, son of William Duncan and Margaret McMurde was born in 1700 in Dunfries, Prince William, Virginia. He died in May 1777 in Snow Creek, Surry, North Carolina. He married **Mary Ann Durron** in 1730 in Prince William, Virginia.

209.   **Mary Ann Durron** was born in 1705 in Prince William, Virginia. She died in May 1777 in Snow Creek, Surry, North Carolina.

Mary Ann Durron and Marshall Duncan had the following children:

104.   i.   James Duncan, son of Marshall Duncan and Mary Ann Durron was born in 1755 in Rowan, Surry, North Carolina (Stokes county was formed in 1789 from Surry Co.). He died in 1840 in Salisbury, Sangamon, Illinois. He married Averilla "Ava" Shelton, daughter of John Shelton and Elizabeth Lawson in 1774 in North Carolina. She was born in 1755 in Surry, North Carolina. She died in 1834 in Salisbury, Sangamon, Illinois.

ii.   Thomas Duncan, son of Marshall Duncan and Mary Ann Durron was born about 1745 in Rowan, North Carolina. He died in 1836 in Stokes County, North Carolina.

iii.   Robert Duncan, son of Marshall Duncan and Mary Ann Durron was born about 1751 in Surry, North Carolina. He died after 1776.

iv.   Charles Duncan, son of Marshall Duncan and Mary Ann Durron was born in May 1748 in Rowan County, North Carolina. He died on 30 May 1818 in Knob Creek, Washington, Tennessee.

v.   Joseph Duncan, son of Marshall Duncan and Mary Ann Durron was born about 1747 in Rowan, Surry, North Carolina. He died in 1828 in Allen, Simpson, Kentucky.

vi.   Marshall Duncan, son of Marshall Duncan and Mary Ann Durron was born in 1739 in Prince William, Virginia. He died about 1815 in Shelby County, Kentucky.

vii.   John Duncan, son of Marshall Duncan and Mary Ann Durron was born in 1730 in Prince William Co, Virginia. He died on 1793 Dec in Sullivan County, Tenneessee.

viii.   Mary Ann Duncan, daughter of Marshall Duncan and Mary Ann Durron was born about 1735 in Prince William, Virginia. She died after 1776 in Rowan, Surry County, North Carolina.

ix.   Rice (Or Reis) Durroon Duncan, son of Marshall Duncan and Mary Ann Durron was born about 1743 in Rowan, North Carolina. He died about 1777 in Washington County, Tennessee.

x.   William Duncan, son of Marshall Duncan and Mary Ann Durron was born about 1737 in Prince William, Virginia. He died after 1797 in Rowan, North Carolina.

210.   **John Shelton** was born on 19 Jul 1722 in Middlesex, Virginia. He died in 1803 in Rockingham county, North Carolina. He married **Elizabeth Lawson**.

211.   **Elizabeth Lawson**, daughter of David Lawson and Frances was born in 1740 in Virginia. She died in 1801 in Madison County, Kentucky.

Elizabeth Lawson and John Shelton had the following child:

105.   i.   Averilla "Ava" Shelton, daughter of John Shelton and Elizabeth Lawson was born in 1755 in Surry, North Carolina. She died in 1834 in Salisbury, Sangamon, Illinois. She married James Duncan, son of Marshall Duncan and Mary Ann Durron in 1774 in North Carolina. He was born in 1755 in Rowan, Surry, North Carolina (Stokes county was formed in 1789 from Surry Co.). He died in 1840 in Salisbury, Sangamon, Illinois.

220.   **Peter Antle**, son of Henry Antil and Margery Smith was born in 1718 in Minchinhampton, Gloucestershire, England. He died on 06 Mar 1771 in Winchester, Frederick, Virginia. He married **Ann ??**.

221.   **Ann ??** was born in 1727 in England?. She died in 1787 in Winchester, Frederick, Virginia.

Ann ?? and Peter Antle had the following children:

110.   i.   Henry Antle Sr., son of Peter Antle and Ann ?? was born in 1753 in Bullskin Run, Frederick, Virginia. He died in 1805 in Cumberland, Kentucky. He married Mary "Polly" Abrell, daughter of John Abrell and Anna Maria Lang in 1771 in Winchester, Frederick, Virginia. She was born in 1752 in Green, Forest, Pennsylvania. She died on 15 Aug 1823 in Sangamon, Illinois.

        ii.   Jacob Antle, son of Peter Antle and Ann ?? was born in 1755 in Bullskin Run, Frederick, Virginia. He died on 11 Aug 1800 in Louisville, Henry, Kentucky. He married Dorcas Dawkins. She was born in 1763. She died in 1843.

        iii.   Ruth Antle, daughter of Peter Antle and Ann ?? was born on 05 Jan 1751 in Openquon Comm, Frederick, Virginia, USA. She died on 05 Jan 1842 in Russell, Kentucky, USA.

        iv.   Christine Antle, daughter of Peter Antle and Ann ?? was born in 1759 in Winchester, Frederick, Virginia, USA. She died in 1830 in Fayette, Ohio, USA.

        v.   Peter Antle, son of Peter Antle and Ann ?? was born in 1757 in Winchester, Frederick, Virginia, USA. He died in 1840.

        vi.   Cynthia Ann Antle.

222.   **John Abrell** was born on 17 Dec 1720 in Zürich, Zurich, Switzerland. He died on 06 Jun 1772 in Berkeley, South Carolina. He married **Anna Maria Lang**.

223.   **Anna Maria Lang**, daughter of Hans Jacob Lang and Anna Meyer was born on 31 Jul 1729 in Stadel, Zurich, Switzerland. She died in Orangeburng, South Carolina.

Anna Maria Lang and John Abrell had the following child:

111.   i.   Mary "Polly" Abrell, daughter of John Abrell and Anna Maria Lang was born in 1752 in Green, Forest, Pennsylvania. She died on 15 Aug 1823 in Sangamon, Illinois. She married Henry Antle Sr., son of Peter Antle and Ann ?? in 1771 in Winchester, Frederick, Virginia. He was born in 1753 in Bullskin Run, Frederick, Virginia. He died in 1805 in Cumberland, Kentucky. She married an unknown spouse in 1771 in Winchester, Frederick, Virginia, USA.

280. **Johan Peter Lenhart**, son of Johann Christopfell Lenhart and Anna Eva Kessler was born on 04 May 1708 in Horn, Rhein-Hunsruck-Kreis, Rheinland-Pfalz, Germany. He died on 04 Apr 1774 in Dover, York, Pennsylvania. He married **Maria Margaretha** in 1732 in Rheinland-Pfalz, Germany.

281. **Maria Margaretha** was born on 28 Sep 1715 in Zweibrücken, Zweibrucken, Rheinland-Pfalz, Germany. She died on 01 Jul 1777 in Dover, York, Pennsylvania.

Maria Margaretha and Johan Peter Lenhart had the following children:

    i.   Godfrey Lenhart, son of Johan Peter Lenhart and Maria Margaretha was born in 1754. He died in 1819.

    ii.   Frederick Lenhart, son of Johan Peter Lenhart and Maria Margaretha was born in 1752.

    iii.   Johan Christopher Lenhart, son of Johan Peter Lenhart and Maria Margaretha was born on 30 Jan 1750 in Greenwich, Berks, Pennsylvania. He died in May 1814 in Addison, Somerset, Pennsylvania.

    iv.   William Lenhart, son of Johan Peter Lenhart and Maria Margaretha was born on 22 Nov 1745. He died on 09 Sep 1818 in Dover, York, Pennsylvania.

    v.   Johan Peter Lenhart Jr., son of Johan Peter Lenhart and Maria Margaretha was born in 1744 in Pennsylvania. He died in 1813.

140.   vi.   Christian Lenhart, son of Johan Peter Lenhart and Maria Margaretha was born in 1722 in Germany. He died on 15 Apr 1810 in Wilkens Twp, Allegheny, Pennsylvania. He married Anna Maria Heindler, daughter of Johan Adam Heindler on 05 Jun 1764 in York, Pennsylvania. She was born in 1740 in Germany. She died on 09 Feb 1827 in Wilkins, Allegheny, Pennsylvania.

    vii.   Maria Magdalena Lenhart, daughter of Johan Peter Lenhart and Maria Margaretha was born in 1732 in York, Pennsylvania, USA. She died on 04 May 1820 in Fairfield, Ohio, USA.

    viii.   Anna Margaret Lenhart, daughter of Johan Peter Lenhart and Maria Margaretha was born in 1732 in Zweibrucken, Rhineland-Palatinate, Germany. She died in 1810 in Somerset, Pennsylvania, USA.

    ix.   Jacob Lenhart, son of Johan Peter Lenhart and Maria Margaretha was born on 18 Nov 1736 in Greenwich, Berks, Pennsylvania, USA. He died on 03 Aug 1793 in Greenwich, Berks, Pennsylvania, USA.

    x.   Philip Lenhart, son of Johan Peter Lenhart and Maria Margaretha was born in 1734 in Berks, Pennsylvania, USA. He died in 1803 in Greenwich, Berks, Pennsylvania, USA.

xi.   Johan George Lenhart, son of Johan Peter Lenhart and Maria Margaretha was born in 1738 in Somerset, Pennsylvania, USA. He died in 1797 in Somerset, Pennsylvania, USA.

xii.   Henry Lenhart, son of Johan Peter Lenhart and Maria Margaretha was born in 1742 in Germany, Adams, Pennsylvania, USA. He died on 21 Mar 1837 in Somerset, Pennsylvania, USA.

xiii.   Jon Christopher Lenhart, son of Johan Peter Lenhart and Maria Margaretha was born in 1740 in Westmoreland, Pennsylvania, USA. He died in 1813 in Unity, Westmoreland, Pennsylvania, USA.

xiv.   Christina Magdalena Lenhart, daughter of Johan Peter Lenhart and Maria Margaretha was born in 1728. She died in 1820.

282.   **Johan Adam Heindler** was born in 1720 in Germany. He died in 1790 in Pennsylvania.

Johan Adam Heindler had the following child:

141.   i.   Anna Maria Heindler, daughter of Johan Adam Heindler was born in 1740 in Germany. She died on 09 Feb 1827 in Wilkins, Allegheny, Pennsylvania. She married Christian Lenhart, son of Johan Peter Lenhart and Maria Margaretha on 05 Jun 1764 in York, Pennsylvania. He was born in 1722 in Germany. He died on 15 Apr 1810 in Wilkens Twp, Allegheny, Pennsylvania.

284.   **Heinrich Baughman**, son of Johann George Bachmann and Anna Maria Schnebelli was born in Jan 1717 in Ibersheim, Worms, Rheinland-Pfalz, Germany. He died on 30 Dec 1769 in Upper Saucon, Northampton, Pennsylvania. He married **Anne** in 1747.

285.   **Anne** was born in 1718 in Germany. She died in 1758 in Montgomery, Pennsylvania.

Anne and Heinrich Baughman had the following children:

142.   i.   Heinrich Baughman Jr., son of Heinrich Baughman and Anne was born in 1742 in Hamburg, Germany. He died on 18 May 1814 in North Huntingdon, Westmoreland, Pennsylvania, United States. He married Anna Catherina Kunkle, daughter of Johannes Kunkle and Anna Magdalena Kaiser in 1764 in Montgomery, Pennsylvania. She was born on 25 Sep 1745 in Fleorsbach, Geinhausen, Hessen, Germany. She died on 10 May 1814 in Irwin, Westmoreland, Pennsylvania.

ii.   Johann Baughman, son of Heinrich Baughman and Anne was born in 1730 in Germany. He died on 09 Dec 1819 in Hempfield, Westmoreland, Pennsylvania, USA.

iii.   Heinrich Baughman, son of Heinrich Baughman and Anne was born in 1742 in Hessen-Kassel, Germany. He died on 18 May 1816 in Irwin, Westmoreland, Pennsylvania, USA.

iv.   Anna Catherine Baughman, daughter of Heinrich Baughman and Anne was born in Germany, Hessen, Germany.

286. **Johannes Kunkle**, son of Johann Sebastian Kunkle and Anna Catharina Samer was born on 21 Sep 1703 in Florsbach, Gelnhausen, Hessen, Germany. He died in 1774 in North Hampton Co., Pennsylvania. He married **Anna Magdalena Kaiser**.

287. **Anna Magdalena Kaiser** was born in 1711 in Gelnhausen, Main-Kinzig-Kreis, Hessen, Germany. She died in 1798 in North Hampton Co., Pennsylvania.

Anna Magdalena Kaiser and Johannes Kunkle had the following children:

    i.   Johannes Hans Jr Kunkle, son of Johannes Kunkle and Anna Magdalena Kaiser was born on 02 Jan 1733 in Gelnhausen, Main-Kinzig-Kreis, Hessen, Germany. He died in Dec 1813 in Hempfield, Westmoreland, Pennsylvania, United States.

    ii.   Peter Kunkel, son of Johannes Kunkle and Anna Magdalena Kaiser was born on 23 Jul 1735 in Floersbach, Geinhausen, Hessen, Germany. He died on 27 Mar 1796 in Colebrookedale, Berks, Pennsylvania, United States.

    iii.   Lorenz Lawrence Kunkle, son of Johannes Kunkle and Anna Magdalena Kaiser was born on 03 Feb 1738 in Gelnhausen, Main-Kinzig-Kreis, Hessen, Germany. He died on 15 Oct 1800 in Hamilton Twp Northampton Co, PA now Monroe, Colorado, United States.

    iv.   Johann Michael Kunkle, son of Johannes Kunkle and Anna Magdalena Kaiser was born on 18 Jun 1743 in Floersbach, Hessen, Germany. He died in Aug 1796 in Washington, Westmoreland, Pennsylvania, United States.

    v.   Christina Kunkel, daughter of Johannes Kunkle and Anna Magdalena Kaiser was born in 1748 in Hamilton, Northampton, Pennsylvania, United States. She died on 24 Nov 1827 in Lehigh, Pennsylvania, United States.

    vi.   Henry Kunkle, son of Johannes Kunkle and Anna Magdalena Kaiser was born in 1750 in Hamilton, Northampton, Pennsylvania, United States.

    vii.   Johann Adam Kunkel, son of Johannes Kunkle and Anna Magdalena Kaiser was born on 15 Jul 1750 in Hamilton, Northampton, Pennsylvania, United States. He died on 24 Nov 1827 in Lehigh, Pennsylvania, United States.

143.   viii.   Anna Catherina Kunkle, daughter of Johannes Kunkle and Anna Magdalena Kaiser was born on 25 Sep 1745 in Fleorsbach, Geinhausen, Hessen, Germany. She died on 10 May 1814 in Irwin, Westmoreland, Pennsylvania. She married Heinrich Baughman Jr., son of Heinrich Baughman and Anne in 1764 in Montgomery, Pennsylvania. He was born in 1742 in Hamburg, Germany. He died on 18 May 1814 in North Huntingdon, Westmoreland, Pennsylvania, United States.

    ix.   Annakina Kunkel, daughter of Johannes Kunkle and Anna Magdalena Kaiser was born on 06 Jun 1753 in Hamilton, Northampton, Pennsylvania, United States. She died in 1800 in Hamilton, Northampton, Pennsylvania, United States.

x.	Johann Michael Kunkle, son of Johannes Kunkle and Anna Magdalena Kaiser was born on 09 Mar 1763 in Bethel, Berks, Pennsylvania, United States.

384.	**Mathias Joachim,** son of Phillip Jochem was born in 1699 in Edigheim, Bayern, Germany. He died on 08 Feb 1783 in Muddy Creek, Greenbrier, West Virginia. He married **Maria Barbara Uhngefehr** on 18 Feb 1721 in Edigheim, Bayern, Germany.

385.	**Maria Barbara Uhngefehr** was born in 1698 in Edigheim, Bayern, Germany. She died in 1730 in Died at sea.

Maria Barbara Uhngefehr and Mathias Joachim had the following children:
i.	Philipp Paul Yoakum, son of Mathias Joachim and Maria Barbara Uhngefehr was born in 1723 in Edigheim, Bayern, Germany. He died on 28 Mar 1807 in Grant, West Virginia. He married Elizabeth Harness, daughter of Michael Peter Harness and Elizabeth Jephe Westfall in 1750 in Hardy, Bedford, Virginia, United States. She was born in 1727 in Bards, Berks, Pennsylvania. She died on 25 Mar 1804 in Pansy, Grant, West Virginia.

192.	ii.	Valentine "Felty" Yoakum, son of Mathias Joachim and Maria Barbara Uhngefehr was born on 08 Sep 1722 in Edigheim, Bayern, Germany. He died on 17 Jul 1763 in Muddy Creek Massacre, Greenbrier, Virginia. He married Margaret See, daughter of Johann George Zeh Jr. and Mary Margaret Tschudi in 1748 in Hardy, West Virginia. She was born in 1725 in Mohawk, Schoharie, New York. She died on 11 Mar 1815 in Franklin, Coshocton, Ohio.

386.	**Johann George Zeh Jr.** was born in 1688 in Ruhlsheim, Bayern, Germany. He died on 23 Apr 1751 in Moorefield, Hardy, West Virginia.

387.	**Mary Margaret Tschudi,** daughter of Jakob Von Tschudi and Elsbeth Schwab was born in 1684 in Frenkendorf, Basel-Country, Switzerland. She died on 14 Feb 1758 in Hampshire, Virginia.

Mary Margaret Tschudi and Johann George Zeh Jr. had the following children:
i.	Elizabeth See, daughter of Johann George Zeh Jr. and Mary Margaret Tschudi was born in 1736 in Tulpehocken Creek, Berks, Pennsylvania, United States. She died in 1811 in Hardy, West Virginia, United States.

ii.	Mary Magdalena See, daughter of Johann George Zeh Jr. and Mary Margaret Tschudi was born in 1738 in Tulpehochen Creek, Berks, Pennsylvania, USA. She died in 1785 in Virginia, USA.

iii.	Frederick Michael See, son of Johann George Zeh Jr. and Mary Margaret Tschudi was born in 1712 in Schoharie, New York. He died on 14 Jul 1763 in Muddy Creek Massacre, Greenbrier, Virginia (Buried at Muddy Creek Presbyterian Cemetery, Greenbriar County, West Virginia). He married Catherine Vanderpool, daughter of Wynant Van Der Poel and Catherina De Hooges in 1744 in Warwick, New Jersey. She was born on 30 Jun 1725 in Albany County, New York. She died in 1806 in Conesville, Coshocton County, Ohio (Buried in William Robinson Family Cemetery. Also known as Thomas Farm Cemetery. Coshocton, OH).

iv.	John Bernhard See, son of Johann George Zeh Jr. and Mary Margaret Tschudi was born in 1714 in Schoharie, Schoharie, New York. He died on 19 Aug 1756 in August, Virginia.

v.	Michael Adam See, son of Johann George Zeh Jr. and Mary Margaret Tschudi was born in 1730 in Silesia, Germany. He died on 03 Jul 1795 in Hardy, Bedford, Virginia, United States.

vi.	George See, son of Johann George Zeh Jr. and Mary Margaret Tschudi was born in 1732 in Silesia, Germany. He died on 11 Jun 1811 in Sumner Summers, Virginia.

193.	vii.	Margaret See, daughter of Johann George Zeh Jr. and Mary Margaret Tschudi was born in 1725 in Mohawk, Schoharie, New York. She died on 11 Mar 1815 in Franklin, Coshocton, Ohio. She married Valentine "Felty" Yoakum, son of Mathias Joachim and Maria Barbara Uhngefehr in 1748 in Hardy, West Virginia. He was born on 08 Sep 1722 in Edigheim, Bayern, Germany. He died on 17 Jul 1763 in Muddy Creek Massacre, Greenbrier, Virginia.

388.	**Peter Van Bibber Sr.**, son of Isaac Jacob Van Bibber and Frances Schumaker was born on 25 May 1695 in Cecil, Maryland. He died on 06 Apr 1769 in Lunenburg, Lunenburg, Virginia. He married **Ann Honriette Gooding** in 1720 in Maryland.

389.	**Ann Honriette Gooding** was born in 1718 in Maryland. She died in 1769 in Virginia.

Ann Honriette Gooding and Peter Van Bibber Sr. had the following children:

194.	i.	Rev. Isaac Michael Van Bibber Sr., son of Peter Van Bibber Sr. and Ann Honriette Gooding was born on 02 Feb 1724 in Strasburg, Chester, Pennsylvania. He died on 10 Oct 1774 in Battle of Point Pleasant, Mason, West Virginia (died in battle). He married Sarah Davis in 1750 in North Carolina. She was born in 1725 in Strasburg, Chester, Pennsylvania. She died on 05 Jan 1800 in Greenbrier, Virginia.

ii.	Captain John Van Bibber, son of Peter Van Bibber Sr. and Ann Honriette Gooding was born on 07 Jan 1732 in Lebanon County, Pennsylvania. He died in 1820 in Point Pleasant, Mason, West Virginia. He married Chloe Staniford about 1765 in Baltimore County, Maryland.

iii.	Peter Van Bibber Jr., son of Peter Van Bibber Sr. and Ann Honriette Gooding was born in 1738 in Lancaster, Pennsylvania. He died on 10 Oct 1796 in Mason, Fairfax, Virginia. He married Margary Bounds in 1756 in Lunenburg, Virginia. She was born in 1740 in Dorchester, Maryland. She died in 1844 in Green City, Hickory, Missouri.

iv.	Brigetta Van Bibber.

400.	**Robert Thomas Stewart** was born about 1696 in Clough, Antrim, Ireland. He died in Clough, Antrim, Ireland.

401.	**Rachel Maxwell** was born in Sep 1700 in Scotland. She died in Ireland.

Rachel Maxwell and Robert Thomas Stewart had the following child:

200.   i.   Rev. William M. Stewart, son of Robert Thomas Stewart and Rachel Maxwell was born in 1722 in Clough, Antrim, Ireland. He died in 1804 in Adams, Brown, Ohio. He married Ann Park on 07 Jul 1762 in Clough, Antrim, Ireland. She was born in 1725 in Clough, Antrim, Ireland. She died in 1787 in Cumberland Valle, Fayette, Pennsylvania.

406.   **Daniel Bradley,** son of Daniel Bradley and Esther Burr was born on 20 May 1729 in Fairfield, Connecticut. He died on 13 Dec 1780 in Fairfield, Connecticut.

407.   **Margaret.**

Margaret and Daniel Bradley had the following child:

203.   i.   Mary Bradley, daughter of Daniel Bradley and Margaret was born on 14 Oct 1752 in Connecticut. She died on 12 Oct 1821 in Palmyra, Washington, Indiana. He was born on 01 May 1749 in Pennsylvania. He died on 25 Dec 1821 in Harrison, Harrison, Indiana.

408.   **William Laughlin** was born in 1700 in Antrim, Antrim, Ireland. He died in Pendleton, Anderson, South Carolina. He married **Nancy Hodges**.

409.   **Nancy Hodges** was born in 1710 in Ireland. She died in Pennsylvania.

Nancy Hodges and William Laughlin had the following child:

204.   i.   John Luke Laughlin Sr., son of William Laughlin and Nancy Hodges was born in 1734 in Antrim, Northern Ireland. He died in 1774 in Pendleton District, South Carolina. He married Mary White, daughter of Anthony White and Mary Ralston in 1759 in Philadelphia, Pennsylvania. She was born in 1745 in Quenbey, Scotland. She died in 1773 in Caldwell County, Kentucky.

410.   **Anthony White** was born about 1700 in Luenberg, Scotland. He married **Mary Ralston**.

411.   **Mary Ralston** was born in Luenberg, Scotland.

Mary Ralston and Anthony White had the following child:

205.   i.   Mary White, daughter of Anthony White and Mary Ralston was born in 1745 in Quenbey, Scotland. She died in 1773 in Caldwell County, Kentucky. She married John Luke Laughlin Sr., son of William Laughlin and Nancy Hodges in 1759 in Philadelphia, Pennsylvania. He was born in 1734 in Antrim, Northern Ireland. He died in 1774 in Pendleton District, South Carolina.

412.   **George Dalrymple,** son of John Dalrymple 1st Earl of Stair and Elizabeth Dundas was born in 1709 in Dalmahoy, Midlothian, Scotland. He died in 1764 in Laurens, South Carolina. He married **Rose Mason,** daughter of John Mason and Eleanor Lewis on 23 Aug 1731 in Philadelphia, Pennsylvania (Married at the First Presbyterian Church of Philadelphia).

413.   **Rose Mason,** daughter of John Mason and Eleanor Lewis was born in 1705 in Philadelphia, Pennsylvania. She died date Unknown in Laurens, South Carolina.

Rose Mason and George Dalrymple had the following children:

206. i. Samuel Dalrymple, son of George Dalrymple and Rose Mason was born in 1755 in Newberry, Newberry, South Carolina. He died in 1791 in Abbeville, Abbeville, South Carolina (Buried at Abbeville, Anderson, SC). He married Sarah Pollock, daughter of James Pollock and Ann Wilson in 1771 in Laurens, Laurens, South Carolina. She was born in 1755 in Pendleton, Anderson, South Carolina. She died in Feb 1837 in Pendleton, Anderson, South Carolina.

ii. Thomas Dalrymple, son of George Dalrymple and Rose Mason was born in 1745 in Philadelphia, Philadelphia, Pennsylvania, United States. He died on 08 Jan 1774 in Craven County, North Carolina, USA.

iii. George Dalrymple, son of George Dalrymple and Rose Mason was born in 1740 in Philadelphia, Philadelphia, Pennsylvania, United States. He died in Jul 1807 in Laurens, Laurens, South Carolina, United States.

iv. John Dalrymple, son of George Dalrymple and Rose Mason was born in 1735 in Newberry, South Carolina. He died on 28 Feb 1798 in Newberry County, South Carolina.

v. Ellinor Dalrymple, daughter of George Dalrymple and Rose Mason was born in 1754 in Newberry, South Carolina.

vi. James Dalrymple, son of George Dalrymple and Rose Mason was born in 1731. He died in 1809.

414. **James Pollock** was born in 1720 in Pennsylvania, Somerset, Pennsylvania. He died in 1793 in Anderson, South Carolina. He married **Ann Wilson**.

415. **Ann Wilson** was born in 1724 in Pennsylvania, Somerset, Pennsylvania. She died in Newberry, South Carolina.

Ann Wilson and James Pollock had the following child:

207. i. Sarah Pollock, daughter of James Pollock and Ann Wilson was born in 1755 in Pendleton, Anderson, South Carolina. She died in Feb 1837 in Pendleton, Anderson, South Carolina. She married Samuel Dalrymple, son of George Dalrymple and Rose Mason in 1771 in Laurens, Laurens, South Carolina. He was born in 1755 in Newberry, Newberry, South Carolina. He died in 1791 in Abbeville, Abbeville, South Carolina (Buried at Abbeville, Anderson, SC).

416. **William Duncan**, son of Rev. William Duncan was born on 01 Oct 1659 in Perth, Perthshire, Scotland. He died in 1720 in Northern Neck, Culpeper, Virginia. He married **Margaret McMurde**.

417. **Margaret McMurde** was born in 1661 in Dumfries-shire, Scotland. She died in 1720 in Bellhaven, Alexandria, Virginia, USA.

Margaret McMurde and William Duncan had the following children:

i. Thomas Duncan, son of William Duncan and Margaret McMurde was born in 1686. He died in 1776.

ii.   Andrew Duncan, son of William Duncan and Margaret McMurde was born in 1694 in Scotland. He died in May 1739 in Londonderry, Rockingham, New Hampshire, United States.

iii.   William Duncan, son of William Duncan and Margaret McMurde was born on 19 Apr 1692 in Perth, Perthshire, Scotland. He died in Oct 1781 in Culpepper, Virginia, United States.

iv.   John Henry Duncan, son of William Duncan and Margaret McMurde was born in 1700 in Dumphries, Scotland. He died in 1793 in United States.

v.   Robert Duncan, son of William Duncan and Margaret McMurde was born in 1696 in Perthshire, Scotland. He died in 1793.

vi.   Townsend Twin Duncan, son of William Duncan and Margaret McMurde was born on 20 Dec 1691 in Perthshire, Scotland.

vii.   James Duncan, son of William Duncan and Margaret McMurde was born on 17 Mar 1689 in Perthshire, Scotland. He died on 25 Oct 1751 in Derry, Lancaster, Pennsylvania, United States.

viii. Mary Twin Duncan, daughter of William Duncan and Margaret McMurde was born on 20 Dec 1691 in Perthshire, Scotland. She died in United States.

208.   ix.   Marshall Duncan, son of William Duncan and Margaret McMurde was born in 1700 in Dunfries, Prince William, Virginia. He died in May 1777 in Snow Creek, Surry, North Carolina. He married Mary Ann Durron in 1730 in Prince William, Virginia. She was born in 1705 in Prince William, Virginia. She died in May 1777 in Snow Creek, Surry, North Carolina. He married an unknown spouse in VA.

x.   Charles II Duncan, son of William Duncan and Margaret McMurde was born on 06 Aug 1687 in Perthshire, Scotland. He died in 1780 in Culpepper, Culpepper, Virginia, United States.

422. **David Lawson**, son of David Lawson was born in 1730 in Bedford, Virginia. He died in 1830 in Stokes, North Carolina. He married **Frances**.

423. **Frances** was born in 1718 in Virginia.

Frances and David Lawson had the following children:

211.   i.   Elizabeth Lawson, daughter of David Lawson and Frances was born in 1740 in Virginia. She died in 1801 in Madison County, Kentucky. She married John Shelton. He was born on 19 Jul 1722 in Middlesex, Virginia. He died in 1803 in Rockingham county, North Carolina. She married an unknown spouse on 30 Jul 1760.

ii.   William Lawson, son of David Lawson and Frances was born in 1759 in Virginia.

iii.   Anne Lawson, daughter of David Lawson and Frances was born in 1757 in

Virginia.

    iv.   Mary Ann Lawson, daughter of David Lawson and Frances was born on 23 Sep 1861 in Tunas, Dallas, Missouri, United States. She died in 1892 in Bartlesville, Washington, Oklahoma, United States.

    v.   David Lawson, son of David Lawson and Frances was born in 1769 in Halifax, Halifax, Virginia, United States. He died in 1840 in Stokes, North Carolina, United States.

    vi.   Aaron Lawson, son of David Lawson and Frances was born in 1763 in Virginia. He died in 1840 in Stokes, North Carolina, United States.

    vii.   James Lawson, son of David Lawson and Frances was born on 31 Jul 1760 in Halifax, Halifax, Virginia, United States. He died in 1830 in Hardin, Kentucky, United States.

    viii.   Elisha Lawson, daughter of David Lawson and Frances was born in 1767 in Halifax, Halifax, Virginia, United States.

    ix.   Elihu Lawson, son of David Lawson and Frances was born in 1766 in Virginia. He died on 10 Jan 1821 in Kentucky, United States.

440. **Henry Antil,** son of James Antill and Frances Burford was born in 1691 in Minchinhampton, Horsley, Gloucestershire, England. He died in 1760 in Frederick, Virginia. He married **Margery Smith.**

441. **Margery Smith** was born in 1695 in England. She died in 1718 in Virginia.

Margery Smith and Henry Antil had the following child:

    220.   i.   Peter Antle, son of Henry Antil and Margery Smith was born in 1718 in Minchinhampton, Gloucestershire, England. He died on 06 Mar 1771 in Winchester, Frederick, Virginia. He married Ann ??. She was born in 1727 in England?. She died in 1787 in Winchester, Frederick, Virginia.

446. **Hans Jacob Lang,** son of Jakob Lang and Elsbeth Muller was born on 28 Nov 1686 in Ober Raat, Stadel Parish, Zurich, Switzerland. He died on 24 Jan 1740 in Raat, Zurich, Switzerland. He married **Anna Meyer,** daughter of Jugli Meyer and Elsbeth Huber on 05 Dec 1717 in Stadel, Zurich, Switzerland.

447. **Anna Meyer,** daughter of Jugli Meyer and Elsbeth Huber was born on 13 May 1697 in Raat, Zurich, Switzerland. She died on 24 Jan 1740 in Switzerland.

Anna Meyer and Hans Jacob Lang had the following children:

    223.   i.   Anna Maria Lang, daughter of Hans Jacob Lang and Anna Meyer was born on 31 Jul 1729 in Stadel, Zurich, Switzerland. She died in Orangeburng, South Carolina. She married John Abrell. He was born on 17 Dec 1720 in Zürich, Zurich, Switzerland. He died on 06 Jun 1772 in Berkeley, South Carolina.

ii.   Anna (Twin) Lang, daughter of Hans Jacob Lang and Anna Meyer was born in
1727. She died on 15 Feb 1728.

iii.   Barbara Lang, daughter of Hans Jacob Lang and Anna Meyer was born in 1733.
She died on 06 Sep 1733.

iv.   Margreth Lang, daughter of Hans Jacob Lang and Anna Meyer was born in 1730.
She died on 14 Sep 1734.

v.   Heinrich Twin Lang, son of Hans Jacob Lang and Anna Meyer was born in 1727.
He died on 14 Aug 1727.

vi.   Johann Lang, son of Hans Jacob Lang and Anna Meyer was born in 1725. He died
on 28 Sep 1728.

vii.   Felix Lang, son of Hans Jacob Lang and Anna Meyer was born in 1724. He died on
20 Aug 1784.

viii. Esther Lang, daughter of Hans Jacob Lang and Anna Meyer was born in 1721.

ix.   Hans Ulrich Lang, son of Hans Jacob Lang and Anna Meyer was born in 1718. He
died on 19 Aug 1719.

x.   Jakob Lang, son of Hans Jacob Lang and Anna Meyer was born on 01 Dec 1737 in
Stadel, Zurich, Switzerland. He died on 03 Aug 1786 in Crims Creek, Newberry,
South Carolina, United States.

Generation 10

560.   **Johann Christopfell Lenhart**, son of Hans Velten Leonhardt and Anna Catherina Schell was
born in 1670 in Benzweiler, Rhein-Hunsruck-Kreis, Rheinland-Pfalz, Germany. He died on 16
Mar 1756 in Klosterkumbd, Rhein-Hunsruck-Kreis, Rheinland-Pfalz, Germany. He married
Anna Eva Kessler.

561.   **Anna Eva Kessler**, daughter of Hans Peter Kessler and Anna Christina Peters was born on 21
Mar 1674 in Rheinland-Pfalz, Germany. She died on 30 Jan 1743 in Horn, Lower Austria,
Austria.

Anna Eva Kessler and Johann Christopfell Lenhart had the following children:

i.   Juliana Leonhardt, daughter of Johann Christopfell Lenhart and Anna Eva Kessler
was born in 1698. She died on 13 Oct 1705 in Klosterkumbd,
Rhein-Hunsruck-Kreis, Rheinland-Pfalz, Germany.

280.   ii.   Johan Peter Lenhart, son of Johann Christopfell Lenhart and Anna Eva Kessler
was born on 04 May 1708 in Horn, Rhein-Hunsruck-Kreis, Rheinland-Pfalz,
Germany. He died on 04 Apr 1774 in Dover, York, Pennsylvania. He married Maria
Margaretha in 1732 in Rheinland-Pfalz, Germany. She was born on 28 Sep 1715 in
Zweibrücken, Zweibrucken, Rheinland-Pfalz, Germany. She died on 01 Jul 1777 in
Dover, York, Pennsylvania.

568. **Johann George Bachmann**, son of Jodocus Bachman and Regula Treichler was born on 02 May 1686 in Richterswil, Canton, Zurich, Switzerland. He died on 19 Nov 1753 in Upper Saucon, Lehigh, Pennsylvania. He married **Anna Maria Schnebelli**, daughter of Johannes Jacob Schnebelli and Elisabeth in 1715 in Ibersheim, Worms, Rheinhessen-Pfalz, Rheinland-Pfalz, Germany.

569. **Anna Maria Schnebelli**, daughter of Johannes Jacob Schnebelli and Elisabeth was born on 12 Apr 1698 in Ibersheim, Worms, Rheinland-Pfalz, Germany. She died on 04 Nov 1776 in Upper Saucon, Lehigh, Pennsylvania (Age at Death: 78).

Anna Maria Schnebelli and Johann George Bachmann had the following children:

    i.   Hans Jacob Bachman, son of Johann George Bachmann and Anna Maria Schnebelli was born on 15 Jan 1720 in Ibersheimerhof, , Rheinland-Pfalz, Germany. He died on 11 Nov 1788 in Lower Saucon, Northampton, Pennsylvania, United States.

    ii.   Mary Bachman, daughter of Johann George Bachmann and Anna Maria Schnebelli was born on 28 Jan 1728 in Coopersburg, Lehigh, Pennsylvania, United States. She died on 01 Sep 1785 in Upper Milford, Lehigh, Pennsylvania, United States.

    iii.   Christian Bachman, son of Johann George Bachmann and Anna Maria Schnebelli was born on 19 May 1727 in Lower Saucon, Northampton, Pennsylvania, United States. He died on 23 Aug 1783 in Lower Milford, Lehigh, Pennsylvania, United States.

    iv.   Elizabeth Bachman, daughter of Johann George Bachmann and Anna Maria Schnebelli was born on 03 Jul 1732 in Coopersburg, Lehigh, Pennsylvania, United States. She died on 15 May 1812 in Plumstead, Bucks, Pennsylvania, United States.

    v.   Johannes Bachman, son of Johann George Bachmann and Anna Maria Schnebelli was born on 01 Aug 1735 in Coopersburg, Lehigh, Pennsylvania, United States. He died on 04 Oct 1805 in Upper Saucon, Lehigh, Pennsylvania, United States.

    vi.   Gristal Bachman, son of Johann George Bachmann and Anna Maria Schnebelli was born on 19 May 1727 in Coopersburg, Lehigh, Pennsylvania, United States.

284.   vii.   Heinrich Baughman, son of Johann George Bachmann and Anna Maria Schnebelli was born in Jan 1717 in Ibersheim, Worms, Rheinland-Pfalz, Germany. He died on 30 Dec 1769 in Upper Saucon, Northampton, Pennsylvania. He married Anne in 1747. She was born in 1718 in Germany. She died in 1758 in Montgomery, Pennsylvania.

    viii.   Johan Jacob BACHMANN, son of Johann George Bachmann and Anna Maria Schnebelli was born in 1719.

    ix.   Susannah Bachman, daughter of Johann George Bachmann and Anna Maria

Schnebelli was born on 17 Apr 1742 in Saucon Tonwship, Lehigh, Pennsylvania, United States. She died in 1742 in Upper Saucon, Lehigh, Pennsylvania, United States.

> x. Abraham Bachman, son of Johann George Bachmann and Anna Maria Schnebelli was born on 12 Nov 1744 in Coopersburg, Lehigh, Pennsylvania, United States. He died on 28 Aug 1825 in Easton, Northampton, Pennsylvania, United States.

> xi. Samuel Bachman, son of Johann George Bachmann and Anna Maria Schnebelli was born on 14 Jan 1739 in Coopersburg, Lehigh, Pennsylvania, United States. He died on 15 Sep 1814 in Sullivan, Tennessee, United States.

> xii. Catherine Bachman, daughter of Johann George Bachmann and Anna Maria Schnebelli was born on 25 Aug 1722 in Saucon, Lehigh, Pennsylvania, United States. She died on 17 Aug 1810 in Montgomery, Montgomery, Pennsylvania, United States.

> xiii. Hans George Bachman, son of Johann George Bachmann and Anna Maria Schnebelli was born on 30 Nov 1724 in Saucon, Lehigh, Pennsylvania, United States. He died on 14 Apr 1806 in Upper Saucon, Northampton, Pennsylvania, United States.

572. **Johann Sebastian Kunkle** was born on 18 Feb 1675 in Gelnhausen, Main-Kinzig-Kreis, Hessen, Germany. He died on 14 Oct 1737 in Gelnhausen, Main-Kinzig-Kreis, Hessen, Germany. He married **Anna Catharina Samer**.

573. **Anna Catharina Samer** was born on 10 Dec 1677 in Gelnhausen, Main-Kinzig-Kreis, Hessen, Germany. She died on 04 Mar 1744 in Gelnhausen, Main-Kinzig-Kreis, Hessen, Germany.

Anna Catharina Samer and Johann Sebastian Kunkle had the following child:

> 286. i. Johannes Kunkle, son of Johann Sebastian Kunkle and Anna Catharina Samer was born on 21 Sep 1703 in Florsbach, Gelnhausen, Hessen, Germany. He died in 1774 in North Hampton Co., Pennsylvania. He married Anna Magdalena Kaiser. She was born in 1711 in Gelnhausen, Main-Kinzig-Kreis, Hessen, Germany. She died in 1798 in North Hampton Co., Pennsylvania.

768. **Phillip Jochem** was born in Mors, Germany.

Phillip Jochem had the following child:

> 384. i. Mathias Joachim, son of Phillip Jochem was born in 1699 in Edigheim, Bayern, Germany. He died on 08 Feb 1783 in Muddy Creek, Greenbrier, West Virginia. He married Eleanor See, daughter of Johann George Zeh Sr. and Anna Magadalena in 1727. She was born in 1710 in Silesia, Germany. She died on 18 Feb 1783 in Will, Lincoln, Kentucky. He married Maria Barbara Uhngefehr on 18 Feb 1721 in Edigheim, Bayern, Germany. She was born in 1698 in Edigheim, Bayern, Germany. She died in 1730 in Died at sea.

774. **Jakob Von Tschudi,** son of Martin Von Tschudi and Margred Grufin Brevin was born on 09 Aug 1635 in Frenkendorf, Basel-Landschaft, Switzerland. He died in 1727 in Frenkendorf,

Basel-Landschaft, Switzerland. He married **Elsbeth Schwab**, daughter of Niclaus Schaub and Barbara Marti on 30 May 1671 in Frenkendorf, Basel-Country, Switzerland.

775. **Elsbeth Schwab**, daughter of Niclaus Schaub and Barbara Marti was born on 08 Jan 1636 in Frenkendorf, Basel-Landschaft, Switzerland. She died date Unknown in Frenkendorf, Basel-Landschaft, Switzerland.

Elsbeth Schwab and Jakob Von Tschudi had the following child:

387. i. Mary Margaret Tschudi, daughter of Jakob Von Tschudi and Elsbeth Schwab was born in 1684 in Frenkendorf, Basel-Country, Switzerland. She died on 14 Feb 1758 in Hampshire, Virginia. He was born in 1688 in Ruhlsheim, Bayern, Germany. He died on 23 Apr 1751 in Moorefield, Hardy, West Virginia.

776. **Isaac Jacob Van Bibber**, son of Jacob Isaac Van Bibber and Christina Hermania was born in 1661 in Duchy of Cleves, Utretch, Netherlands. He died on 14 Sep 1723 in Cecil County, Maryland. He married **Frances Schumaker** on 25 May 1690 in Pennsylvania.

777. **Frances Schumaker** was born in 1669 in St. Stephen's Parish.

Frances Schumaker and Isaac Jacob Van Bibber had the following children:

i. Christiana Van Bibber, daughter of Isaac Jacob Van Bibber and Frances Schumaker was born on 15 Aug 1698 in St. Stephen's Parish, Cecil County, MD.

ii. Jacob Van Bibber, son of Isaac Jacob Van Bibber and Frances Schumaker was born on 26 Oct 1691 in St. Stephen's Parish, Cecil County, MD. He died on 14 Aug 1733.

iii. Veronica Van Bibber, daughter of Isaac Jacob Van Bibber and Frances Schumaker was born on 26 Oct 1692 in St. Stephen's Parish, Cecil County, MD.

388. iv. Peter Van Bibber Sr., son of Isaac Jacob Van Bibber and Frances Schumaker was born on 25 May 1695 in Cecil, Maryland. He died on 06 Apr 1769 in Lunenburg, Lunenburg, Virginia. He married Ann Honriette Gooding in 1720 in Maryland. She was born in 1718 in Maryland. She died in 1769 in Virginia.

v. Hester Van Bibber, daughter of Isaac Jacob Van Bibber and Frances Schumaker was born on 09 May 1693 in St. Stephen's Parish, Cecil County, MD.

vi. Issac Van Bibber, son of Isaac Jacob Van Bibber and Frances Schumaker was born on 15 Jul 1701 in St. Stephen's Parish, Cecil County, MD.

812. **Daniel Bradley**, son of Daniel Bradley and Abigail Jackson was born on 11 Jun 1704 in Fairfield, Connecticut. He died on 23 Apr 1765 in Ridgefield, Fairfield, Connecticut. He married **Esther Burr**, daughter of Daniel Burr and Elizabeth Pinckney on 11 Jun 1724 in Fairfield, Connecticut.

813. **Esther Burr**, daughter of Daniel Burr and Elizabeth Pinckney was born on 31 Jan 1703 in Fairfield, Connecticut. She died on 29 Dec 1741 in Ridgefield, Fairfield, Connecticut.

Esther Burr and Daniel Bradley had the following child:

| 406. | i. | Daniel Bradley, son of Daniel Bradley and Esther Burr was born on 20 May 1729 in Fairfield, Connecticut. He died on 13 Dec 1780 in Fairfield, Connecticut. |

824. **John Dalrymple 1st Earl of Stair**, son of Sir James Dalrymple 1st Viscount of Stair and Margaret Ross was born in 1648 in Stair, Kyle, Ayrshire, Scotland. He died on 08 Jan 1707 in Edinburgh, Midlothian, Scotland. He married **Elizabeth Dundas**, daughter of Sir John Dundas 9th of Newliston Craigton and Duddingston and Agnes Gray on 19 Jan 1669 in Scotland.

825. **Elizabeth Dundas**, daughter of Sir John Dundas 9th of Newliston Craigton and Duddingston and Agnes Gray was born in 1650 in Newliston, West Lothian, Scotland. She died on 25 May 1731 in Edinburgh, Midlothian, Scotland.

Notes for John Dalrymple 1st Earl of Stair:
John Dalrymple
http://trees.ancestry.com/rd?f=image&guid=f57ea38f-b92f-4e6a-bf52-4c6761c3a189&tid=251
61444&pid=278

Elizabeth Dundas and John Dalrymple 1st Earl of Stair had the following children:

412.	i.	George Dalrymple, son of John Dalrymple 1st Earl of Stair and Elizabeth Dundas was born in 1709 in Dalmahoy, Midlothian, Scotland. He died in 1764 in Laurens, South Carolina. He married Rose Mason, daughter of John Mason and Eleanor Lewis on 23 Aug 1731 in Philadelphia, Pennsylvania (Married at the First Presbyterian Church of Philadelphia). She was born in 1705 in Philadelphia, Pennsylvania. She died date Unknown in Laurens, South Carolina.
	ii.	James Dalrymple, son of John Dalrymple 1st Earl of Stair and Elizabeth Dundas was born on 19 Feb 1669. He died on 26 Feb 1667 in Edinburgh, Bartholomew, Indiana, United States.
	iii.	William Dalrymple, son of John Dalrymple 1st Earl of Stair and Elizabeth Dundas was born in 1678 in Sanquar, Dumfries-shire, Scotland. He died on 03 Dec 1744.
	iv.	Margaret Dalrymple, daughter of John Dalrymple 1st Earl of Stair and Elizabeth Dundas was born on 04 Feb 1677 in Greenock, Renfrewshire, Scotland. She died on 03 Apr 1777.
	v.	James Dalrymple, son of John Dalrymple 1st Earl of Stair and Elizabeth Dundas was born on 24 Jun 1676. He died on 30 Nov 1760 in Wigton, Manchester, Jamaica.
	vi.	Earl Stair, son of John Dalrymple 1st Earl of Stair and Elizabeth Dundas was born on 20 Jul 1673 in Edinburgh, Bartholomew, Indiana, United States. He died on 09 May 1747 in Edinburgh, Bartholomew, Indiana, United States.
	vii.	John Dalrymple, son of John Dalrymple 1st Earl of Stair and Elizabeth Dundas was born on 20 Jul 1673 in Newliston, Linlithgowshire, Scotland. He died on 09 May 1747 in Queensberry House, Edinburgh.

viii. James Dalrymple, son of John Dalrymple 1st Earl of Stair and Elizabeth Dundas was born on 19 Feb 1669. He died on 30 Nov 1760 in Wigton, Manchester, Jamaica.

ix. Elizabeth Dalrymple, daughter of John Dalrymple 1st Earl of Stair and Elizabeth Dundas was born in 1687.

x. George DALRYMPLE, son of John Dalrymple 1st Earl of Stair and Elizabeth Dundas was born on 10 May 1680. He died on 29 Jul 1745 in Moffat, Dumfries-shire, Scotland.

xi. Agnes Dalrymple, daughter of John Dalrymple 1st Earl of Stair and Elizabeth Dundas was born on 03 May 1675 in Scotland.

826. **John Mason** was born in 1735 in Berkeley, South Carolina. He died on 15 Nov 1783 in Indian Creek, Berkeley, South Carolina.

827. **Eleanor Lewis** was born in 1740 in Berkeley, South Carolina. She died in 1783 in South Carolina.

Eleanor Lewis and John Mason had the following child:

413. i. Rose Mason, daughter of John Mason and Eleanor Lewis was born in 1705 in Philadelphia, Pennsylvania. She died date Unknown in Laurens, South Carolina. She married George Dalrymple, son of John Dalrymple 1st Earl of Stair and Elizabeth Dundas on 23 Aug 1731 in Philadelphia, Pennsylvania (Married at the First Presbyterian Church of Philadelphia). He was born in 1709 in Dalmahoy, Midlothian, Scotland. He died in 1764 in Laurens, South Carolina.

832. **Rev. William Duncan**, son of John Duncan and Janet Macarthur was born on 07 Jan 1630 in Perth, Perthshire, Scotland. He died on 02 Jan 1692 in Glasgow, Lanarkshire, Scotland.

Rev. William Duncan and Susan Haldane had the following children:

i. Thomas Duncan. He died in 1776 in Cumberland, Pennsylvania.

ii. Susan Duncan, daughter of Rev. William Duncan and Susan Haldane was born on 28 Jan 1665 in Perthshire, Scotland.

iii. Mary Duncan, daughter of Rev. William Duncan and Susan Haldane was born on 01 Feb 1667 in Perthshire, Scotland. She died in Northern Neck, Virginia, United States.

iv. George Duncan, son of Rev. William Duncan and Susan Haldane was born in 1661 in Perth, Perthshire, Scotland. He died in United States.

v. Henry Duncan, son of Rev. William Duncan and Susan Haldane was born on 14 Jan 1663 in Perth, Perthshire, Scotland. He died in Westmoreland, Westmoreland, Virginia, United States.

Rev. William Duncan had the following child:

416. i. William Duncan, son of Rev. William Duncan was born on 01 Oct 1659 in Perth, Perthshire, Scotland. He died in 1720 in Northern Neck, Culpeper, Virginia. He married Margaret McMurde. She was born in 1661 in Dumfries-shire, Scotland. She died in 1720 in Bellhaven, Alexandria, Virginia, USA.

844. **David Lawson** was born in 1710 in Bedford, Virginia. He died in 1803 in Virginia.

David Lawson had the following children:

422. i. David Lawson, son of David Lawson was born in 1730 in Bedford, Virginia. He died in 1830 in Stokes, North Carolina. He married Frances. She was born in 1718 in Virginia.

ii. James Lawson, son of David Lawson was born in 1734 in Patrick, Virginia, USA.

iii. John Isham Lawson, son of David Lawson was born in 1740 in Bedford, Virginia, USA. He died on 19 Mar 1813 in Stokes, North Carolina, USA.

iv. William Lawson, son of David Lawson was born in 1732 in Bedford, Virginia, USA. He died in 1799.

v. Bartholomew Bartlett Lawson, son of David Lawson was born in 1727 in Lunenburg, Virginia, USA. He died on 25 Aug 1782 in Virginia, USA.

vi. Elizabeth Lawson, daughter of David Lawson was born in 1740 in Virginia, USA. She died in 1801 in Madison, Kentucky, USA.

vii. James Lawson, son of David Lawson was born on 31 Jul 1760 in St James Northam, Goochland, Virginia, USA. He died in 1830 in Hardin, Kentucky, USA.

880. **James Antill,** son of Richard Antille was born on 30 Mar 1660 in Horsley, Gloucestershire, England. He died in 1755 in Virginia. He married **Frances Burford,** daughter of Thomas Justice Burford and Ann Pope on 30 Mar 1689.

881. **Frances Burford,** daughter of Thomas Justice Burford and Ann Pope was born in 1660 in Marlyand.

Frances Burford and James Antill had the following child:

440. i. Henry Antil, son of James Antill and Frances Burford was born in 1691 in Minchinhampton, Horsley, Gloucestershire, England. He died in 1760 in Frederick, Virginia. He married Margery Smith. She was born in 1695 in England. She died in 1718 in Virginia.

892. **Jakob Lang,** son of Junghans Lang and Elsbeth Surber was born on 04 Mar 1660 in Stadel, Zurich, Switzerland. He died on 19 Jul 1720 in Raat, Zurich, Switzerland. He married **Elsbeth Muller** on 01 Nov 1681 in Stadel Parish, Zurich, Switzerland.

893. **Elsbeth Muller** was born on 30 Aug 1657 in Nassenbail, Niedechasli, Switzerland. She died on 14 Jun 1715 in Raat, Zurich, Switzerland.

Elsbeth Muller and Jakob Lang had the following child:

446.   i.   Hans Jacob Lang, son of Jakob Lang and Elsbeth Muller was born on 28 Nov 1686 in Ober Raat, Stadel Parish, Zurich, Switzerland. He died on 24 Jan 1740 in Raat, Zurich, Switzerland. He married Anna Meyer, daughter of Jugli Meyer and Elsbeth Huber on 05 Dec 1717 in Stadel, Zurich, Switzerland. She was born on 13 May 1697 in Raat, Zurich, Switzerland. She died on 24 Jan 1740 in Switzerland.

894.   **Jugli Meyer** was born in 1671 in Raat, Zurich, Switzerland. He married **Elsbeth Huber**.

895.   **Elsbeth Huber** was born in 1675 in Raat, Zurich, Switzerland. She died on 29 Jan 1731 in Riffersevel, Switzerland.

Elsbeth Huber and Jugli Meyer had the following child:

447.   i.   Anna Meyer, daughter of Jugli Meyer and Elsbeth Huber was born on 13 May 1697 in Raat, Zurich, Switzerland. She died on 24 Jan 1740 in Switzerland. She married Hans Jacob Lang, son of Jakob Lang and Elsbeth Muller on 05 Dec 1717 in Stadel, Zurich, Switzerland. He was born on 28 Nov 1686 in Ober Raat, Stadel Parish, Zurich, Switzerland. He died on 24 Jan 1740 in Raat, Zurich, Switzerland.

Generation 11

1120.   **Hans Velten Leonhardt**, son of Johann Conrad Leonardt and Arlene Lenhart was born date Unknown in Zweibrücken, Zweibrucken, Rheinland-Pfalz, Germany. He died on 23 Jan 1716 in Benzweiler, Rhein-Hunsruck-Kreis, Rheinland-Pfalz, Germany. He married **Anna Catherina Schell** in 1674.

1121.   **Anna Catherina Schell** was born in 1648 in Mörschbach, Rhein-Hunsruck-Kreis, Rheinland-Pfalz, Germany. She died on 13 Jan 1733 in Benzweiler, Rhein-Hunsruck-Kreis, Rheinland-Pfalz, Germany.

Anna Catherina Schell and Hans Velten Leonhardt had the following children:

560.   i.   Johann Christopfell Lenhart, son of Hans Velten Leonhardt and Anna Catherina Schell was born in 1670 in Benzweiler, Rhein-Hunsruck-Kreis, Rheinland-Pfalz, Germany. He died on 16 Mar 1756 in Klosterkumbd, Rhein-Hunsruck-Kreis, Rheinland-Pfalz, Germany. He married Anna Eva Kessler. She was born on 21 Mar 1674 in Rheinland-Pfalz, Germany. She died on 30 Jan 1743 in Horn, Lower Austria, Austria. He married Anna Eva Kessler on 10 Nov 1693 in Horn, Rhein-Hunsruck-Kreis, Rheinland-Pfalz, Germany. She was born on 21 Mar 1674 in Rheinland-Pfalz, Germany. She died on 30 Jan 1743 in Klosterkumbd, Rhein-Hunsruck-Kreis, Rheinland-Pfalz, Germany.

     ii.   Anna Maria Lenhardt, daughter of Hans Velten Leonhardt and Anna Catherina Schell was born in 1666.

     iii.   Johannes Peter Leonhardt.

     iv.   Johan Valentin Leonhardt, son of Hans Velten Leonhardt and Anna Catherina Schell was born in 1668.

1122.   **Hans Peter Kessler**, son of Johannes Kessler and Katharina Hipp was born in 1640 in

Klosterkumbd, Rhein-Hunsruck-Kreis, Rheinland-Pfalz, Germany. He died on 12 May 1694 in Klosterkumbd, Rhein-Hunsruck-Kreis, Rheinland-Pfalz, Germany. He married **Anna Christina Peters** on 13 Oct 1663 in Horn, Rhein-Hunsruck-Kreis, Rheinland-Pfalz, Germany.

1123. **Anna Christina Peters** was born in 1640 in Klosterkumbd, Rhein-Hunsruck-Kreis, Rheinland-Pfalz, Germany. She died on 26 May 1694 in Klosterkumbd, Rhein-Hunsruck-Kreis, Rheinland-Pfalz, Germany.

Anna Christina Peters and Hans Peter Kessler had the following children:

       i.   Elisabeth Catharina Kessler, daughter of Hans Peter Kessler and Anna Christina Peters was born on 14 Jul 1678 in Germany.

       ii.   Christopher Kessler, son of Hans Peter Kessler and Anna Christina Peters was born on 25 Feb 1672 in Klosterkumbd, Rhein-Hunsruck-Kreis, Rheinland-Pfalz, Germany. He died on 26 Oct 1696 in Klosterkumbd, Rhein-Hunsruck-Kreis, Rheinland-Pfalz, Germany.

561.   iii.   Anna Eva Kessler, daughter of Hans Peter Kessler and Anna Christina Peters was born on 21 Mar 1674 in Rheinland-Pfalz, Germany. She died on 30 Jan 1743 in Horn, Lower Austria, Austria. She married Johann Christopfell Lenhart. He was born in 1670 in Benzweiler, Rhein-Hunsruck-Kreis, Rheinland-Pfalz, Germany. He died on 16 Mar 1756 in Klosterkumbd, Rhein-Hunsruck-Kreis, Rheinland-Pfalz, Germany.

       iv.   Anna Gertraud Kessler, daughter of Hans Peter Kessler and Anna Christina Peters was born on 18 Oct 1664 in Klosterkumbd, Rhein-Hunsruck-Kreis, Rheinland-Pfalz, Germany.

       v.   Agnes Margaretha Kessler, daughter of Hans Peter Kessler and Anna Christina Peters was born on 26 Mar 1670.

       vi.   Anna Catharina Kessler, daughter of Hans Peter Kessler and Anna Christina Peters was born on 28 Aug 1664 in Germany.

1136. **Jodocus Bachman**, son of Hans Jacob Bachman and Regula Strickler was born on 03 Aug 1657 in Richterswil, Zurich Canton, Switzerland. He died on 19 Aug 1736 in Richterswil, Zurich Canton, Switzerland. He married **Regula Treichler**, daughter of Heinrich Treichler and Dorothea Hiestand on 12 Feb 1677 in Richterswil,Zurich Canton,,Switzerland.

1137. **Regula Treichler**, daughter of Heinrich Treichler and Dorothea Hiestand was born in 1646 in Richterswil, Zurich Canton, Switzerland. She died on 26 Jan 1706 in Richterswil, Zurich Canton, Switzerland.

Regula Treichler and Jodocus Bachman had the following children:

       i.   Jorgli Bachman, son of Jodocus Bachman and Regula Treichler was born on 08 Mar 1679 in Switzerland. He died in 1680.

       ii.   Georg Bachman, son of Jodocus Bachman and Regula Treichler was born on 03 Mar 1678 in Richterswil, Zurich, Switzerland. He died on 14 Sep 1735 in United

States.

     iii.   Elsbeth Bachman, daughter of Jodocus Bachman and Regula Treichler was born on 10 Aug 1683 in Ibersheim, Worms, Rheinland-Pfalz, Germany. She died on 04 Oct 1757 in Richterswil, Zurich, Switzerland.

     iv.   Hans Heinrich Bachman, son of Jodocus Bachman and Regula Treichler was born on 14 Feb 1685 in Ibersheim, Worms, Rheinland-Pfalz, Germany. He died on 22 Nov 1753.

568.   v.   Johann George Bachmann, son of Jodocus Bachman and Regula Treichler was born on 02 May 1686 in Richterswil, Canton, Zurich, Switzerland. He died on 19 Nov 1753 in Upper Saucon, Lehigh, Pennsylvania. He married Anna Maria Schnebelli, daughter of Johannes Jacob Schnebelli and Elisabeth in 1715 in Ibersheim, Worms, Rheinhessen-Pfalz, Rheinland-Pfalz, Germany. She was born on 12 Apr 1698 in Ibersheim, Worms, Rheinland-Pfalz, Germany. She died on 04 Nov 1776 in Upper Saucon, Lehigh, Pennsylvania (Age at Death: 78). He married ESTHER OBERHOLTZER on 16 Nov 1748 in Lehigh, Pennsylvania. She was born on 16 May 1728 in Deep Run, Bucks, Pennsylvania, United States. She died in 1812 in now, Lehigh, Pennsylvania, United States.

1138. **Johannes Jacob Schnebelli**. He married **Elisabeth**.

1139. **Elisabeth**.

Elisabeth and Johannes Jacob Schnebelli had the following child:

569.   i.   Anna Maria Schnebelli, daughter of Johannes Jacob Schnebelli and Elisabeth was born on 12 Apr 1698 in Ibersheim, Worms, Rheinland-Pfalz, Germany. She died on 04 Nov 1776 in Upper Saucon, Lehigh, Pennsylvania (Age at Death: 78). She married Johann George Bachmann, son of Jodocus Bachman and Regula Treichler in 1715 in Ibersheim, Worms, Rheinhessen-Pfalz, Rheinland-Pfalz, Germany. He was born on 02 May 1686 in Richterswil, Canton, Zurich, Switzerland. He died on 19 Nov 1753 in Upper Saucon, Lehigh, Pennsylvania.

1548. **Martin Von Tschudi,** son of Hans Von Tschudi and Elsbeth Gyger was born on 27 Apr 1591 in Basel, Basel Town, Switzerland. He died in 1637 in Frankendorf, Basel, Switzerland. He married **Margred Grufin Brevin** on 03 Oct 1614 in Hunzah, Basel, Switzerland.

1549. **Margred Grufin Brevin** was born in Mar 1591 in Lausen, Basel, Switzerland. She died on 18 Mar 1665 in Frankendorf, Canton Basel, Switzerland.

Margred Grufin Brevin and Martin Von Tschudi had the following children:

     i.   Chrischona Tschudi, daughter of Martin Von Tschudi and Margred Grufin Brevin was born on 07 Oct 1632 in Frenkendorf, Basel-Country, Switzerland. She died on 12 Dec 1688.

     ii.   Heinrich Tschudi, son of Martin Von Tschudi and Margred Grufin Brevin was born on 16 Jan 1627 in Frenkendorf, Basel-Country, Switzerland. He died on 04 Nov 1629 in Frenkendorf, Basel-Country, Switzerland.

iii.   Martin Tschudi, son of Martin Von Tschudi and Margred Grufin Brevin was born
       on 19 Jan 1622 in Frenkendorf, Basel-Country, Switzerland.

iv.   Margarethe Tschudi, daughter of Martin Von Tschudi and Margred Grufin Brevin
       was born on 01 Aug 1624 in Frenkendorf, Basel-Country, Switzerland.

v.   Hans Jacob Tschudi, son of Martin Von Tschudi and Margred Grufin Brevin was
       born on 28 Nov 1619 in Frenkendorf, Basel-Country, Switzerland. He died on 27
       Nov 1629.

vi.   Anna Tschudi, daughter of Martin Von Tschudi and Margred Grufin Brevin was
       born in 1616 in Frenkendorf, Basel-Country, Switzerland. She died on 27 Nov
       1629.

774.   vii.   Jakob Von Tschudi, son of Martin Von Tschudi and Margred Grufin Brevin was
              born on 09 Aug 1635 in Frenkendorf, Basel-Landschaft, Switzerland. He died in
              1727 in Frenkendorf, Basel-Landschaft, Switzerland. He married Elsbeth Schwab,
              daughter of Niclaus Schaub and Barbara Marti on 30 May 1671 in Frenkendorf,
              Basel-Country, Switzerland. She was born on 08 Jan 1636 in Frenkendorf,
              Basel-Landschaft, Switzerland. She died date Unknown in Frenkendorf,
              Basel-Landschaft, Switzerland.

1550. Niclaus Schaub. He married **Barbara Marti**, daughter of Laurentz Marti on 27 Feb 1638 in
Basel, Basel Town, Switzerland.

1551. Barbara Marti.

Barbara Marti and Niclaus Schaub had the following child:

775.   i.   Elsbeth Schwab, daughter of Niclaus Schaub and Barbara Marti was born on 08
              Jan 1636 in Frenkendorf, Basel-Landschaft, Switzerland. She died date Unknown
              in Frenkendorf, Basel-Landschaft, Switzerland. She married Jakob Von Tschudi,
              son of Martin Von Tschudi and Margred Grufin Brevin on 30 May 1671 in
              Frenkendorf, Basel-Country, Switzerland. He was born on 09 Aug 1635 in
              Frenkendorf, Basel-Landschaft, Switzerland. He died in 1727 in Frenkendorf,
              Basel-Landschaft, Switzerland.

1552. Jacob Isaac Van Bibber, son of Isaac Jacobs VanBebber and Hester Op Den Graeff was born
about 1643 in Duchy of Cleves, Utretch, Netherlands (born 1630 in Krefeld (Germany) Holland).
He died on 07 Sep 1705 in Germantown, Pennsylvania (Buried in the floor of St. Stephen's
Church, Earlsville, MD). He married **Christina Hermania** in 1660 in Krefeld, Krefeld,
Nordrhein-Westfalen, Germany.

1553. Christina Hermania was born in 1643 in Duchy of Cleves, Utretch, Netherlands. She died on 05
Sep 1711 in Philadelphia, Pennsylvania (Buried at St. Stephen's Episcopal Church, Earlsville,
MD).

Christina Hermania and Jacob Isaac Van Bibber had the following children:

776.   i.   Isaac Jacob Van Bibber, son of Jacob Isaac Van Bibber and Christina Hermania

was born in 1661 in Duchy of Cleves, Utretch, Netherlands. He died on 14 Sep 1723 in Cecil County, Maryland. He married Frances Schumaker on 25 May 1690 in Pennsylvania. She was born in 1669 in St. Stephen's Parish.

ii.   Henry Van Bibber, son of Jacob Isaac Van Bibber and Christina Hermania was born in Utrecht, Netherlands. He died in 1733 in Cecil County, Maryland, USA.

iii.   Deborah Van Bibber, daughter of Jacob Isaac Van Bibber and Christina Hermania was born in 1660. She died in 1727 in Bohemia Manor, Maryland.

iv.   Margaryte Van Bibber.

v.   Lisbet Van Bibber, daughter of Jacob Isaac Van Bibber and Christina Hermania was born about 1646 in Krefeld, Krefeld, Nordrhein-Westfalen, Germany. She died in 1684.

vi.   Matthias Van Bibber, son of Jacob Isaac Van Bibber and Christina Hermania was born date Unknown. He died on 03 Aug 1739.

1624. **Daniel Bradley**, son of Francis Bradley Sr. and Ruth Barlow was born in 1673 in Fairfield, Connecticut. He died on 01 Jul 1713 in Fairfield, Connecticut. He married **Abigail Jackson**, daughter of Joseph Jackson and Mary Godwin in 1697.

1625. **Abigail Jackson**, daughter of Joseph Jackson and Mary Godwin was born in 1676 in Fairfield, Connecticut. She died in 1714 in Fairfield, Connecticut.

Abigail Jackson and Daniel Bradley had the following child:

812.   i.   Daniel Bradley, son of Daniel Bradley and Abigail Jackson was born on 11 Jun 1704 in Fairfield, Connecticut. He died on 23 Apr 1765 in Ridgefield, Fairfield, Connecticut. He married Esther Burr, daughter of Daniel Burr and Elizabeth Pinckney on 11 Jun 1724 in Fairfield, Connecticut. She was born on 31 Jan 1703 in Fairfield, Connecticut. She died on 29 Dec 1741 in Ridgefield, Fairfield, Connecticut.

1626. **Daniel Burr**, son of Jehu Burr Jr. and Esther Ward was born in 1660 in Fairfield, Connecticut. He died on 01 Aug 1727 in Fairfield, Connecticut. He married **Elizabeth Pinckney**.

1627. **Elizabeth Pinckney**, daughter of Phillip Pinckney and Jane Phippen was born in 1675 in Fairfield, Connecticut. She died in 1722 in Fairfield, Connecticut.

Elizabeth Pinckney and Daniel Burr had the following children:

813.   i.   Esther Burr, daughter of Daniel Burr and Elizabeth Pinckney was born on 31 Jan 1703 in Fairfield, Connecticut. She died on 29 Dec 1741 in Ridgefield, Fairfield, Connecticut. She married Daniel Bradley, son of Daniel Bradley and Abigail Jackson on 11 Jun 1724 in Fairfield, Connecticut. He was born on 11 Jun 1704 in Fairfield, Connecticut. He died on 23 Apr 1765 in Ridgefield, Fairfield, Connecticut.

      ii.   Rev. Aaron Burr, son of Daniel Burr and Elizabeth Pinckney was born on 04 Jan 1716 in Princeton, Mercer, New Jersey, USA. He died on 24 Sep 1757 in Fairfield,

Connecticut. He married Esther Edwards. She was born on 13 Feb 1732. She died on 07 Apr 1758.

1648.   **Sir James Dalrymple 1st Viscount of Stair**, son of James Dalrymple and Janet Kennedy was born in May 1619 in Barr, Ayrshire, Scotland. He died on 29 Nov 1695 in St Giles Cathedral, Edinburgh, Midlothian, Scotland. He married **Margaret Ross**, daughter of James Ross and Sarah Syme on 21 Sep 1643 in Scotland.

1649.   **Margaret Ross**, daughter of James Ross and Sarah Syme was born in 1623 in Balneil, Wigtownshire, Scotland. She died in 1692 in Edinburgh, Midlothian, Scotland.

Notes for Sir James Dalrymple 1st Viscount of Stair:
Sir James Dalrymple-1st Viscount of Stair
http://trees.ancestry.com/rd?f=image&guid=4c14c169-060e-4de3-b571-23172190fc35&tid=251
61444&pid=291

Notes for Margaret Ross:
Ross Family Crest
http://trees.ancestry.com/rd?f=image&guid=85084796-db26-49a7-bd00-db6d4a760c3d&tid=2
5161444&pid=290

Margaret Ross and Sir James Dalrymple 1st Viscount of Stair had the following children:

i. Sarah DALRYMPLE, daughter of Sir James Dalrymple 1st Viscount of Stair and Margaret Ross was born on 19 Nov 1654 in Stair, Ayrshire, Scotland. She died on 03 Dec 1744.

ii. Janet DALRYMPLE, daughter of Sir James Dalrymple 1st Viscount of Stair and Margaret Ross was born in 1654 in Scotland. She died in 1669 in Scotland.

iii. Isobel Dalrymple, daughter of Sir James Dalrymple 1st Viscount of Stair and Margaret Ross was born on 30 Jan 1659 in Stair, Ayrshire, Scotland. She died in 1698.

iv. David DALRYMPLE, son of Sir James Dalrymple 1st Viscount of Stair and Margaret Ross was born in 1655 in Drummerchie, Aryshire, Scotland. He died in 1721 in Scotland.

v. Thomas Dalrymple, son of Sir James Dalrymple 1st Viscount of Stair and Margaret Ross was born in 1650 in Killoch, Scotland. He died in May 1719 in Scotland.

vi. James Dalrymple, son of Sir James Dalrymple 1st Viscount of Stair and Margaret Ross was born in 1644 in Borthwick, Midlothian, Scotland. He died on 08 Sep 1720 in Borthwick, Midlothian, Scotland.

vii.   Jean Dalrymple.

viii.   Janet Dalrymple, daughter of Sir James Dalrymple 1st Viscount of Stair and Margaret Ross was born in 1681. She died on 26 Dec 1726 in Midlothia, Scotland.

ix.   Elizabeth DALRYMPLE, daughter of Sir James Dalrymple 1st Viscount of Stair and Margaret Ross was born on 09 Oct 1653 in Stair, Ayrshire, Scotland. She died on 21 Mar 1733.

x.   Hew Dalrymple, son of Sir James Dalrymple 1st Viscount of Stair and Margaret Ross was born in 1652 in North Berwick, East Lothian, Scotland. He died in 1736 in Scotland.

xi.   Baronet Sir, son of Sir James Dalrymple 1st Viscount of Stair and Margaret Ross was born in 1648 in Kyle, Ayrshire, Scotland. He died on 08 Jan 1705 in Edinburgh, Midlothian, Scotland.

xii.   Margaret Dalrymple, daughter of Sir James Dalrymple 1st Viscount of Stair and Margaret Ross was born on 30 Jan 1659 in Stair, Ayrshire, Scotland. She died in 1698.

xiii.   Hugh Dalrymple, son of Sir James Dalrymple 1st Viscount of Stair and Margaret Ross was born in 1652 in North Berwick, East Lothian, Scotland. He died on 01 Feb 1737 in Scotland.

824.   xiv.   John Dalrymple 1st Earl of Stair, son of Sir James Dalrymple 1st Viscount of Stair and Margaret Ross was born in 1648 in Stair, Kyle, Ayrshire, Scotland. He died on 08 Jan 1707 in Edinburgh, Midlothian, Scotland. He married Elizabeth Dundas, daughter of Sir John Dundas 9th of Newliston Craigton and Duddingston and Agnes Gray on 19 Jan 1669 in Scotland. She was born in 1650 in Newliston, West Lothian, Scotland. She died on 25 May 1731 in Edinburgh, Midlothian, Scotland.

1650.   **Sir John Dundas 9th of Newliston Craigton and Duddingston**, son of James Dundas and Lady Elizabeth Douglas was born in 1615 in Kirkliston, West Lothian, Scotland. He died in 1655.

1651.   **Agnes Gray,** daughter of William Gray and Egidia Smith was born on 05 Dec 1622 in Edinburgh, Midlothian, Scotland. She died in 1699 in Edinburgh, Midlothian, Scotland.

Agnes Gray and Sir John Dundas 9th of Newliston Craigton and Duddingston had the following children:

i.   Mary PRIMROSE, daughter of Sir John Dundas 9th of Newliston Craigton and Duddingston and Agnes Gray was born in Aug 1657 in Edinburgh, Midlothian, Scotland.

ii.   Earl of Rosebery, son of Sir John Dundas 9th of Newliston Craigton and Duddingston and Agnes Gray was born on 18 Dec 1664 in Edinburgh, Bartholomew, Indiana, United States. He died on 20 Oct 1723.

iii.	Archibald Primrose, son of Sir John Dundas 9th of Newliston Craigton and Duddingston and Agnes Gray was born on 18 Dec 1664 in Edinburgh, Bartholomew, Indiana, USA. He died on 20 Oct 1723.

iv.	Grizel Primrose, daughter of Sir John Dundas 9th of Newliston Craigton and Duddingston and Agnes Gray was born on 19 Sep 1661.

825.	v.	Elizabeth Dundas, daughter of Sir John Dundas 9th of Newliston Craigton and Duddingston and Agnes Gray was born in 1650 in Newliston, West Lothian, Scotland. She died on 25 May 1731 in Edinburgh, Midlothian, Scotland. She married John Dalrymple 1st Earl of Stair, son of Sir James Dalrymple 1st Viscount of Stair and Margaret Ross on 19 Jan 1669 in Scotland. He was born in 1648 in Stair, Kyle, Ayrshire, Scotland. He died on 08 Jan 1707 in Edinburgh, Midlothian, Scotland.

1664.	**John Duncan**, son of Andrew Duncan and Chippewa Indian was born in 1612 in St Ninians, Stirlingshire, Scotland. He died in 1630 in Dundee, Angus, Scotland. He married **Janet Macarthur**.

1665.	**Janet Macarthur** was born in 1600 in Scotland. She died in Scotland.

Janet Macarthur and John Duncan had the following children:
832.	i.	Rev. William Duncan, son of John Duncan and Janet Macarthur was born on 07 Jan 1630 in Perth, Perthshire, Scotland. He died on 02 Jan 1692 in Glasgow, Lanarkshire, Scotland. He married Susan Haldane on 29 Aug 1657 in Glasgow, Lanarkshire, Scotland. She was born in 1635 in Perth, Perthshire, Scotland. She died in 1669 in Glasgow, Lanarkshire, Scotland.

ii.	Alexander Duncan, son of John Duncan and Janet Macarthur was born in 1629 in Scotland.

1760.	**Richard Antille** was born in 1630 in London, London, England. He died in Horsley, Gloucestershire, England.

Richard Antille had the following child:
880.	i.	James Antill, son of Richard Antille was born on 30 Mar 1660 in Horsley, Gloucestershire, England. He died in 1755 in Virginia. He married Frances Burford, daughter of Thomas Justice Burford and Ann Pope on 30 Mar 1689. She was born in 1660 in Marlyand.

1762.	**Thomas Justice Burford** was born in 1630 in England. He died on 24 Mar 1686 in Charles, Maryland, United States. He married **Ann Pope**.

1763.	**Ann Pope** was born in 1639 in St. Mary's County, Maryland. She died in May 1700 in Charles, Maryland, United States.

Ann Pope and Thomas Justice Burford had the following child:
881.	i.	Frances Burford, daughter of Thomas Justice Burford and Ann Pope was born in 1660 in Marlyand. She married James Antill, son of Richard Antille on 30 Mar 1689. He was born on 30 Mar 1660 in Horsley, Gloucestershire, England. He died

in 1755 in Virginia.

1784. **Junghans Lang**, son of Hans Lang and Margreth Volkhart was born on 11 Feb 1627 in Stadel, Zurich, Switzerland. He died on 26 Jun 1692 in Raat, Zurich, Switzerland. He married **Elsbeth Surber**, daughter of Hans Surber and Elsbeth Kempf on 20 Nov 1645 in Stadel, Zurich, Switzerland.

1785. **Elsbeth Surber**, daughter of Hans Surber and Elsbeth Kempf was born on 07 Jan 1627 in Niederhori, Bulach, Switzerland. She died on 14 Jun 1715 in Raat, Switzerland.

Elsbeth Surber and Junghans Lang had the following child:

892. i. Jakob Lang, son of Junghans Lang and Elsbeth Surber was born on 04 Mar 1660 in Stadel, Zurich, Switzerland. He died on 19 Jul 1720 in Raat, Zurich, Switzerland. He married Elsbeth Muller on 01 Nov 1681 in Stadel Parish, Zurich, Switzerland. She was born on 30 Aug 1657 in Nassenbail, Niedechasli, Switzerland. She died on 14 Jun 1715 in Raat, Zurich, Switzerland.

Generation 12

2240. **Johann Conrad Leonardt**, son of Hanss Leonhardt and Brigida Jacob was born in 1624 in Bilsdorf, Saarlouis, Saarland, Germany. He died in 1695 in Nalbach, Saarlouis, Saarland, Germany. He married **Arlene Lenhart**.

2241. **Arlene Lenhart** was born in 1635 in Bilsdorf, Saarlouis, Saarland, Germany. She died in 1705 in Bilsdorf, Saarlouis, Saarland, Germany.

Arlene Lenhart and Johann Conrad Leonardt had the following child:

1120. i. Hans Velten Leonhardt, son of Johann Conrad Leonardt and Arlene Lenhart was born date Unknown in Zweibrücken, Zweibrucken, Rheinland-Pfalz, Germany. He died on 23 Jan 1716 in Benzweiler, Rhein-Hunsruck-Kreis, Rheinland-Pfalz, Germany. He married Anna Catherina Schell in 1674. She was born in 1648 in Mörschbach, Rhein-Hunsruck-Kreis, Rheinland-Pfalz, Germany. She died on 13 Jan 1733 in Benzweiler, Rhein-Hunsruck-Kreis, Rheinland-Pfalz, Germany.

2244. **Johannes Kessler** was born in 1628 in Tiefenbach, Biberach, Baden-Wuerttemberg, Germany. He died on 06 Feb 1694 in Hart, Memmingen, Bayern, Germany. He married **Katharina Hipp**.

2245. **Katharina Hipp** was born in 1628 in Hungary. She died on 16 Sep 1703 in Hart, Memmingen, Bayern, Germany.

Katharina Hipp and Johannes Kessler had the following child:

1122. i. Hans Peter Kessler, son of Johannes Kessler and Katharina Hipp was born in 1640 in Klosterkumbd, Rhein-Hunsruck-Kreis, Rheinland-Pfalz, Germany. He died on 12 May 1694 in Klosterkumbd, Rhein-Hunsruck-Kreis, Rheinland-Pfalz, Germany. He married Anna Christina Peters on 13 Oct 1663 in Horn, Rhein-Hunsruck-Kreis, Rheinland-Pfalz, Germany. She was born in 1640 in Klosterkumbd, Rhein-Hunsruck-Kreis, Rheinland-Pfalz, Germany. She died on 26 May 1694 in Klosterkumbd, Rhein-Hunsruck-Kreis, Rheinland-Pfalz, Germany.

2272. **Hans Jacob Bachman**, son of Ulrich Bachman and Anna Grog was born in 1629 in Richterswirl, Zurich, Switzerland. He died in 1704 in Richterswirl, Zurich, Switzerland. He married **Regula**

Strickler on 04 Oct 1653 in Richterswil, Zurich, Switzerland.

2273. **Regula Strickler** was born in 1629 in Richterswil, Canton, Zurich, Switzerland. She died on 20 Dec 1679 in Richterswil, Zurich, Switzerland.

Regula Strickler and Hans Jacob Bachman had the following child:

   1136.   i.   Jodocus Bachman, son of Hans Jacob Bachman and Regula Strickler was born on 03 Aug 1657 in Richterswil, Zurich Canton, Switzerland. He died on 19 Aug 1736 in Richterswil, Zurich Canton, Switzerland. He married Regula Treichler, daughter of Heinrich Treichler and Dorothea Hiestand on 12 Feb 1677 in Richterswil,Zurich Canton,,Switzerland. She was born in 1646 in Richterswil, Zurich Canton, Switzerland. She died on 26 Jan 1706 in Richterswil, Zurich Canton, Switzerland.

2274. **Heinrich Treichler** was born in 1603 in Richterswil, Zurich, Switzerland. He died on 07 Mar 1679 in Richterswil, Zurich, Switzerland. He married **Dorothea Hiestand**.

2275. **Dorothea Hiestand** was born in 1607 in Richterswil, Zurich, Switzerland. She died on 13 Jul 1678 in Richterswil, Zurich, Switzerland.

Dorothea Hiestand and Heinrich Treichler had the following child:

   1137.   i.   Regula Treichler, daughter of Heinrich Treichler and Dorothea Hiestand was born in 1646 in Richterswil, Zurich Canton, Switzerland. She died on 26 Jan 1706 in Richterswil, Zurich Canton, Switzerland. She married Jodocus Bachman, son of Hans Jacob Bachman and Regula Strickler on 12 Feb 1677 in Richterswil,Zurich Canton,,Switzerland. He was born on 03 Aug 1657 in Richterswil, Zurich Canton, Switzerland. He died on 19 Aug 1736 in Richterswil, Zurich Canton, Switzerland.

3096. **Hans Von Tschudi**, son of Martin Von Tschudi and Anna Salatine was born on 01 Aug 1563 in Frenkendorf, Canton Basel, Switzerland. He died in 1594 in Frenkendorf, Canton Basel, Switzerland. He married **Elsbeth Gyger**.

3097. **Elsbeth Gyger** was born about 1568 in Giebenach, Canton Basel, Switzerland. She died in 1594 in Frankendorf, Canton Basel, Switzerland.

Elsbeth Gyger and Hans Von Tschudi had the following children:

       i.   Martin Von I Tschudi, son of Hans Von Tschudi and Elsbeth Gyger was born on 06 Jun 1591 in Frenkendorf, Basel-Country, Switzerland. He died on 18 Mar 1664 in Basel, Basel-Town, Switzerland.

       ii.   Anna Tschudi, daughter of Hans Von Tschudi and Elsbeth Gyger was born on 01 Jul 1593 in Frenkendorf, Basel-Country, Switzerland. She died in Frenkendorf, Basel-Country, Switzerland.

       iii.   Bernhard Tschudi, son of Hans Von Tschudi and Elsbeth Gyger was born on 29 May 1597 in Frenkendorf, Basel-Country, Switzerland. He died on 10 Jan 1629.

   1548.   iv.   Martin Von Tschudi, son of Hans Von Tschudi and Elsbeth Gyger was born on 27 Apr 1591 in Basel, Basel Town, Switzerland. He died in 1637 in Frankendorf, Basel, Switzerland. He married Margred Grufin Brevin on 03 Oct 1614 in Hunzah,

Basel, Switzerland. She was born in Mar 1591 in Lausen, Basel, Switzerland. She died on 18 Mar 1665 in Frankendorf, Canton Basel, Switzerland.

3100. **Hans Schaub** was born about 1575 in Basel, Basel Town, Switzerland. He died in 1610 in Ziefen, Basel Town, Switzerland. He married **Adelheit Meyer**.

3101. **Adelheit Meyer** was born about 1575 in Basel, Basel Town, Switzerland.

Adelheit Meyer and Hans Schaub had the following child:

1550.   i.   Niclaus Schaub. He married Barbara Marti, daughter of Laurentz Marti on 27 Feb 1638 in Basel, Basel Town, Switzerland.

3102. **Laurentz Marti** was born about 1575.

Laurentz Marti had the following child:

1551.   i.   Barbara Marti. She married Niclaus Schaub, son of Hans Schaub and Adelheit Meyer on 27 Feb 1638 in Basel, Basel Town, Switzerland.

3104. **Isaac Jacobs VanBebber**, son of Willem VanVredenburg and Dorothea Farrill was born in Dec 1610 in Krefeld, Rhenish, Preussen, Germany. He died in 1690 in Germantown, Pennsylvania. He married **Hester Op Den Graeff**, daughter of Bishop Herman Isacks Op Den Graeff and Grietjen Pletjes in 1629 in Germany.

3105. **Hester Op Den Graeff**, daughter of Bishop Herman Isacks Op Den Graeff and Grietjen Pletjes was born on 18 Jan 1609 in Krefeld, Krefeld, Nordrhein-Westfalen, Germany. She died on 21 Feb 1642 in Germantown, Philadelphia, Pennsylvania.

Hester Op Den Graeff and Isaac Jacobs VanBebber had the following children:

1552.   i.   Jacob Isaac Van Bibber, son of Isaac Jacobs VanBebber and Hester Op Den Graeff was born about 1643 in Duchy of Cleves, Utretch, Netherlands (born 1630 in Krefeld (Germany) Holland). He died on 07 Sep 1705 in Germantown, Pennsylvania (Buried in the floor of St. Stephen's Church, Earlsville, MD). He married Christina Hermania in 1660 in Krefeld, Krefeld, Nordrhein-Westfalen, Germany. She was born in 1643 in Duchy of Cleves, Utretch, Netherlands. She died on 05 Sep 1711 in Philadelphia, Pennsylvania (Buried at St. Stephen's Episcopal Church, Earlsville, MD).

      ii.   Henry VanBebber, son of Isaac Jacobs VanBebber and Hester Op Den Graeff was born in 1640 in Utrecht, Netherlands. He died in 1736 in Bohemia Manor, Cecil, Maryland, United States.

3248. **Francis Bradley Sr.**, son of Thomas Bradley and Francis Savile was born in 1625 in Fairfield, Connecticut. He died on 22 Oct 1698 in Fairfield, Connecticut. He married **Ruth Barlow**.

3249. **Ruth Barlow**, daughter of John Barlow and Ann Ward was born in 1638 in Fairfield, Connecticut. She died on 22 Oct 1689 in Fairfield, Connecticut.

Ruth Barlow and Francis Bradley Sr. had the following children:

1624.   i.   Daniel Bradley, son of Francis Bradley Sr. and Ruth Barlow was born in 1673 in Fairfield, Connecticut. He died on 01 Jul 1713 in Fairfield, Connecticut. He married

Abigail Jackson, daughter of Joseph Jackson and Mary Godwin in 1697. She was born in 1676 in Fairfield, Connecticut. She died in 1714 in Fairfield, Connecticut.

ii.   Abigail Bradley, daughter of Francis Bradley Sr. and Ruth Barlow was born in 1667 in Fairfield, Connecticut. She died in Age, Cuanza Sul, Angola.

iii.   Mary Bradley, daughter of Francis Bradley Sr. and Ruth Barlow was born on 05 Dec 1677 in Fairfield, Connecticut.

iv.   John Bradley, son of Francis Bradley Sr. and Ruth Barlow was born in 1664 in Fairfield, Fairfield, CT. He died on 14 Apr 1703 in Fairfield, Fairfield, CT.

v.   Ruth Bradley, daughter of Francis Bradley Sr. and Ruth Barlow was born in 1662 in Fairfield, Connecticut. She died in 1688 in Fairfield, Connecticut.

vi.   Joseph Bradley, son of Francis Bradley Sr. and Ruth Barlow was born in 1676 in Fairfield, Connecticut. He died on 04 Dec 1716 in Fairfield, Connecticut.

vii.   John Bradley, son of Francis Bradley Sr. and Ruth Barlow was born in 1664 in Fairfield, Connecticut. He died on 14 Apr 1703 in Fairfield, Connecticut.

viii.   Daniel Bradley, son of Francis Bradley Sr. and Ruth Barlow was born on 14 Feb 1662. He died in 1668.

ix.   Joseph Bradley, son of Francis Bradley Sr. and Ruth Barlow was born on 07 Feb 1664. He died in 1668.

3250. **Joseph Jackson** was born in 1649 in Fairfield, Connecticut. He died on 31 Oct 1681 in Fairfield, Connecticut. He married **Mary Godwin**.

3251. **Mary Godwin** was born in 1653 in Fairfield, Connecticut. She died on 28 Jul 1678 in Cohansey, Cumberland, New Jersey.

Mary Godwin and Joseph Jackson had the following child:

1625.   i.   Abigail Jackson, daughter of Joseph Jackson and Mary Godwin was born in 1676 in Fairfield, Connecticut. She died in 1714 in Fairfield, Connecticut. She married Daniel Bradley, son of Francis Bradley Sr. and Ruth Barlow in 1697. He was born in 1673 in Fairfield, Connecticut. He died on 01 Jul 1713 in Fairfield, Connecticut.

3252. **Jehu Burr Jr.,** son of Jehu Burr Sr. and Elizabeth Cable was born in 1625 in Lavenham, Suffolk, England. He died on 31 Oct 1692 in Fairfield, Connecticut. He married **Esther Ward**, daughter of Andrew Ward and Hester Sherman on 20 Oct 1658 in Fairfield, Connecticut.

3253. **Esther Ward**, daughter of Andrew Ward and Hester Sherman was born in 1623 in Watertown, Middlesex, Massachusetts. She died in 1664 in Fairfield, Connecticut.

Esther Ward and Jehu Burr Jr. had the following children:

i.   Sarah Burr, daughter of Jehu Burr Jr. and Esther Ward was born in 1672 in Fairfield, Connecticut. She died on 17 Oct 1711 in Fairfield, Connecticut.

1626.   ii.   Daniel Burr, son of Jehu Burr Jr. and Esther Ward was born in 1660 in Fairfield, Connecticut. He died on 01 Aug 1727 in Fairfield, Connecticut. He married Elizabeth Pinckney. She was born in 1675 in Fairfield, Connecticut. She died in 1722 in Fairfield, Connecticut.

3254. **Phillip Pinckney**, son of Rev. Philip Pinckney and Margaret Gough was born on 07 Mar 1618 in Dinton, Wiltshire, England. He died on 28 Feb 1687 in Eastchester, Westchester, New York. He married **Jane Phippen**, daughter of George Phippen and Joan Rie Penrose on 20 Jun 1648 in Fairfield, Connecticut.

3255. **Jane Phippen**, daughter of George Phippen and Joan Rie Penrose was born in Jan 1629 in England. She died in Feb 1680 in Eastchester, Westchester, New York.

Jane Phippen and Phillip Pinckney had the following children:

1627.   i.   Elizabeth Pinckney, daughter of Phillip Pinckney and Jane Phippen was born in 1675 in Fairfield, Connecticut. She died in 1722 in Fairfield, Connecticut. She married Daniel Burr. He was born in 1660 in Fairfield, Connecticut. He died on 01 Aug 1727 in Fairfield, Connecticut.

   ii.   Jane Pinckney, daughter of Phillip Pinckney and Jane Phippen was born in 1675 in Fairfield, Connecticut. She died in Sep 1714 in Fairfield, Connecticut.

   iii.   Deborah Pinckney, daughter of Phillip Pinckney and Jane Phippen was born in 1668. She died in 1689.

   iv.   Thomas Pinckney, son of Phillip Pinckney and Jane Phippen was born in 1662 in Eastchester, Westchester, New York, United States. He died on 01 Nov 1732 in Mount Vernon, Westchester, New York, United States.

   v.   Rachel Pinckney, daughter of Phillip Pinckney and Jane Phippen was born in 1654 in Fairfield, Connecticut. She died in 1684 in Dorchester, Suffolk, Massachusettes, USA.

   vi.   Hannah Pinckney, daughter of Phillip Pinckney and Jane Phippen was born in 1652 in Fairfield, Connecticut.

   vii.   Abigail Pinckney, daughter of Phillip Pinckney and Jane Phippen was born in 1650 in Fairfield, Connecticut. She died in 1683 in Mount Vernon, Westchester, New York, USA.

   viii.   William Pinkney, son of Phillip Pinckney and Jane Phippen was born in 1663 in Fairfield, Connecticut. He died in 1755 in Eastchester, Westchester, New York, United States.

3296. **James Dalrymple**, son of James Dalrymple and Isabel Kennedy was born in 1589 in Drummurchie, Barr, Ayrshire, Scotland. He died in Jan 1625 in Barr, Ayrshire, Scotland.

3297. **Janet Kennedy**, daughter of Fergus Kennedy was born in 1598 in Knockdaw, Scotland. She died in 1663 in Scotland.

Janet Kennedy and James Dalrymple had the following children:

1648. i. Sir James Dalrymple 1st Viscount of Stair, son of James Dalrymple and Janet Kennedy was born in May 1619 in Barr, Ayrshire, Scotland. He died on 29 Nov 1695 in St Giles Cathedral, Edinburgh, Midlothian, Scotland. He married Margaret Ross, daughter of James Ross and Sarah Syme on 21 Sep 1643 in Scotland. She was born in 1623 in Balneil, Wigtownshire, Scotland. She died in 1692 in Edinburgh, Midlothian, Scotland.

       ii. James 1st Viscount of Stair Dalrymple--32, son of James Dalrymple and Janet Kennedy was born in May 1619 in Barr, Ayrshire, Scotland. He died on 23 Nov 1695 in House, Edinburgh, Mid Lothian, Scotland.

3298. **James Ross**, son of Robert Ross and Jean Hamilton was born in 1589 in Hawkhead, Renfrewshire, Scotland. He died on 17 Dec 1633 in Balneil, Wigtownshire, Scotland. He married **Sarah Syme** in 1613 in Scotland.

3299. **Sarah Syme** was born in 1595. She died in 1623 in Edinburgh, Midlothian, Scotland.

Sarah Syme and James Ross had the following child:

1649. i. Margaret Ross, daughter of James Ross and Sarah Syme was born in 1623 in Balneil, Wigtownshire, Scotland. She died in 1692 in Edinburgh, Midlothian, Scotland. She married Fergus Kennedy on 20 Jan 1639. He was born in 1590 in Knockdaw, Ayrshire, Scotland. He died in 1643 in Down, Ireland. She married Sir James Dalrymple 1st Viscount of Stair, son of James Dalrymple and Janet Kennedy on 21 Sep 1643 in Scotland. He was born in May 1619 in Barr, Ayrshire, Scotland. He died on 29 Nov 1695 in St Giles Cathedral, Edinburgh, Midlothian, Scotland.

3300. **James Dundas**, son of Walter Dundas and Elizabeth Bruce was born in 1600 in Magdalens, Scotland. He died in 1637 in Fermanagh, Ireland.

3301. **Lady Elizabeth Douglas**.

Lady Elizabeth Douglas and James Dundas had the following child:

1650. i. Sir John Dundas 9th of Newliston Craigton and Duddingston, son of James Dundas and Lady Elizabeth Douglas was born in 1615 in Kirkliston, West Lothian, Scotland. He died in 1655. She was born on 05 Dec 1622 in Edinburgh, Midlothian, Scotland. She died in 1699 in Edinburgh, Midlothian, Scotland.

3302. **William Gray**, son of Thomas Gray and Margaret Walker was born in 1600 in Pittendrum, Scotland. He died on 04 Aug 1648 in Edinburgh, Midlothian, Scotland. He married **Egidia Smith** on 20 Jun 1620 in Midlothian, Scotland.

3303. **Egidia Smith** was born in 1603 in Grothill, Midlothian, Scotland. She died on 17 Sep 1686 in Midlothian, Scotland.

Egidia Smith and William Gray had the following children:

1651. i. Agnes Gray, daughter of William Gray and Egidia Smith was born on 05 Dec 1622 in Edinburgh, Midlothian, Scotland. She died in 1699 in Edinburgh, Midlothian,

Scotland. She married Archibald Primrose in 1663 in Edinburgh, Midlothian, Scotland. He was born on 16 May 1616. He died on 27 Nov 1679. He was born in 1615 in Kirkliston, West Lothian, Scotland. He died in 1655. He was born in 1460 in Dundas, Stirlingshire, Scotland. He died in 1495 in Scotland.

    ii.   William Pittendrum Gray, son of William Gray and Egidia Smith was born on 21 Jul 1621 in Bildeston, Suffolk, England. He died in Aug 1660 in Duel, Villach-Land, Karnten, Austria.

    iii.   John Gray, son of William Gray and Egidia Smith was born on 28 Oct 1627.

    iv.   Isobel Gray, daughter of William Gray and Egidia Smith was born in 1638 in Scotland. She died in Oct 1676.

    v.   Andrew Gray, son of William Gray and Egidia Smith was born on 23 Aug 1633. He died on 08 Feb 1656.

    vi.   MARY GRAY, daughter of William Gray and Egidia Smith was born on 02 Apr 1630 in Edinburgh, Midlothian, Scotland. She died on 27 Feb 1668.

3328. Andrew Duncan, son of John Duncan and Jenet Andro was born in 1575 in Perth, Perthshire, Scotland. He died in 1605 in Dauiot, Aberdeenshire, Scotland. He married **Chippewa Indian**.

3329. Chippewa Indian was born in 1580 in United States. She died in 1625 in Scotland.

Chippewa Indian and Andrew Duncan had the following children:

    i.   David Duncan, son of Andrew Duncan and Chippewa Indian was born in 1605.

    ii.   Willliam Duncan, son of Andrew Duncan and Chippewa Indian was born on 11 Sep 1601. He died in 1647.

1664.   iii.   John Duncan, son of Andrew Duncan and Chippewa Indian was born in 1612 in St Ninians, Stirlingshire, Scotland. He died in 1630 in Dundee, Angus, Scotland. He married Janet Macarthur. She was born in 1600 in Scotland. She died in Scotland.

    iv.   Joe Duncan.

3568. Hans Lang, son of Hans Lang and Elsbeth Baumgartner was born on 06 Feb 1588 in Windlach, Zurich, Switzerland. He died on 12 Jul 1663 in Windlach, Zurich, Switzerland. He married **Margreth Volkhart** on 28 Jun 1612 in Stadel Parish, Zurich, Switzerland.

3569. Margreth Volkhart was born in 1591 in Nschikon, Niedechasli, Switzerland. She died on 26 Jan 1651 in Windlach, Zurich, Switzerland.

Margreth Volkhart and Hans Lang had the following child:

1784.   i.   Junghans Lang, son of Hans Lang and Margreth Volkhart was born on 11 Feb 1627 in Stadel, Zurich, Switzerland. He died on 26 Jun 1692 in Raat, Zurich, Switzerland. He married Elsbeth Surber, daughter of Hans Surber and Elsbeth

Kempf on 20 Nov 1645 in Stadel, Zurich, Switzerland. She was born on 07 Jan 1627 in Niederhori, Bulach, Switzerland. She died on 14 Jun 1715 in Raat, Switzerland.

3570. **Hans Surber**, son of Heinrich Surber and Anna Koch was born in 1600 in Switzerland. He died on 21 Aug 1664. He married **Elsbeth Kempf**.

3571. **Elsbeth Kempf** was born in 1602.

Elsbeth Kempf and Hans Surber had the following child:

1785. i. Elsbeth Surber, daughter of Hans Surber and Elsbeth Kempf was born on 07 Jan 1627 in Niederhori, Bulach, Switzerland. She died on 14 Jun 1715 in Raat, Switzerland. She married Junghans Lang, son of Hans Lang and Margreth Volkhart on 20 Nov 1645 in Stadel, Zurich, Switzerland. He was born on 11 Feb 1627 in Stadel, Zurich, Switzerland. He died on 26 Jun 1692 in Raat, Zurich, Switzerland.

Generation 13

4480. **Hanss Leonhardt** was born in 1587 in Bischweiler, Elsass, Germany. He married **Brigida Jacob**.

4481. **Brigida Jacob** was born in 1601 in Bischweiler, Bas-Rhin, Alsace, France.

Brigida Jacob and Hanss Leonhardt had the following child:

2240. i. Johann Conrad Leonardt, son of Hanss Leonhardt and Brigida Jacob was born in 1624 in Bilsdorf, Saarlouis, Saarland, Germany. He died in 1695 in Nalbach, Saarlouis, Saarland, Germany. He married Arlene Lenhart. She was born in 1635 in Bilsdorf, Saarlouis, Saarland, Germany. She died in 1705 in Bilsdorf, Saarlouis, Saarland, Germany. He married Catharina Coning. She was born in 1630. She died on 29 Aug 1703 in Nalbach, Saarlouis, Saarland, Germany.

4544. **Ulrich Bachman** was born in 1600 in Langnau, Canton, Bern, Switzerland. He died in 1661 in Laubersweiler, Canton, Bern, Switzerland. He married **Anna Grog** in 1630.

4545. **Anna Grog** was born in 1605 in Lauperswil, Canton, Bern, Switzerland. She died in 1665 in Zürich, Zurich, Switzerland.

Anna Grog and Ulrich Bachman had the following children:

i. Anna Catharina Bachman, daughter of Ulrich Bachman and Anna Grog was born on 01 Jan 1639 in Laubersweiler, Canton, Bern, Switzerland.

ii. Nicholas Bachman, son of Ulrich Bachman and Anna Grog was born on 28 Jul 1633 in Lauperswil, Canton, Bern, Switzerland. He died in 1700 in Hirschland, Bas-Rhin, Alsace, France.

2272. iii. Hans Jacob Bachman, son of Ulrich Bachman and Anna Grog was born in 1629 in Richterswirl, Zurich, Switzerland. He died in 1704 in Richterswirl, Zurich, Switzerland. He married Regula Strickler on 04 Oct 1653 in Richterswil, Zurich, Switzerland. She was born in 1629 in Richterswil, Canton, Zurich, Switzerland. She died on 20 Dec 1679 in Richterswil, Zurich, Switzerland.

6192. **Martin Von Tschudi**, son of Hans Von Tschudi and Elsa Barth was born in 1537 in Frenkendorf, Liestal, Basel-Landschaft, Switzerland. He died in Frenkendorf, Liestal, Basel-Landschaft, Switzerland. He married **Anna Salatine** in 1560 in Frenkendorf, Basel-Country, Switzerland.

6193. **Anna Salatine** was born in 1541 in Frenkendorf, Basel-Country, Switzerland. She died in Basel, Basel-Town, Switzerland.

Anna Salatine and Martin Von Tschudi had the following child:

3096. i. Hans Von Tschudi, son of Martin Von Tschudi and Anna Salatine was born on 01 Aug 1563 in Frenkendorf, Canton Basel, Switzerland. He died in 1594 in Frenkendorf, Canton Basel, Switzerland. He married Elsbeth Gyger. She was born about 1568 in Giebenach, Canton Basel, Switzerland. She died in 1594 in Frankendorf, Canton Basel, Switzerland. He married an unknown spouse on 11 Feb 1589 in Munzach, Basel, Switzerland.

6208. **Willem VanVredenburg** was born in 1580 in Rotterdam, Rotterdam, Zuid-Holland, Netherlands. He died in 1658 in Holland, Reusel-de Mierden, Noord-Brabant, Netherlands. He married **Dorothea Farrill**.

6209. **Dorothea Farrill** was born in 1585 in Netherlands.

Dorothea Farrill and Willem VanVredenburg had the following child:

3104. i. Isaac Jacobs VanBebber, son of Willem VanVredenburg and Dorothea Farrill was born in Dec 1610 in Krefeld, Rhenish, Preussen, Germany. He died in 1690 in Germantown, Pennsylvania. He married Hester Op Den Graeff, daughter of Bishop Herman Isacks Op Den Graeff and Grietjen Pletjes in 1629 in Germany. She was born on 18 Jan 1609 in Krefeld, Krefeld, Nordrhein-Westfalen, Germany. She died on 21 Feb 1642 in Germantown, Philadelphia, Pennsylvania.

6210. **Bishop Herman Isacks Op Den Graeff**, son of John William De La Marck and Anna Van Aldekerk was born on 26 Nov 1585 in Aldekerk, Kleve, Nordrhein-Westfalen, Germany. He died on 27 Dec 1642 in Krefeld, Krefeld, Nordrhein-Westfalen, Germany. He married **Grietjen Pletjes**, daughter of Driessen Andreas Pletjes and Alet Gobels Syllys on 16 Aug 1605 in Kempen, Heinsberg, Nordrhein-Westfalen, Germany.

6211. **Grietjen Pletjes**, daughter of Driessen Andreas Pletjes and Alet Gobels Syllys was born on 26 Nov 1588 in Kempen, Holland. She died on 17 Jan 1642/43 in Krefeld, Krefeld, Nordrhein-Westfalen, Germany.

Grietjen Pletjes and Bishop Herman Isacks Op Den Graeff had the following child:

3105. i. Hester Op Den Graeff, daughter of Bishop Herman Isacks Op Den Graeff and Grietjen Pletjes was born on 18 Jan 1609 in Krefeld, Krefeld, Nordrhein-Westfalen, Germany. She died on 21 Feb 1642 in Germantown, Philadelphia, Pennsylvania. She married Isaac Jacobs VanBebber, son of Willem VanVredenburg and Dorothea Farrill in 1629 in Germany. He was born in Dec 1610 in Krefeld, Rhenish, Preussen, Germany. He died in 1690 in Germantown, Pennsylvania.

6496. **Thomas Bradley** was born in 1594 in Pomfret, Yorkshire, England. He died in 1636 in England. He married **Francis Savile**.

6497. Francis Savile was born in 1604 in Pomfret, Yorkshire, England. She died on 30 Jan 1663 in Yorkshire, England.

Francis Savile and Thomas Bradley had the following child:

    3248.   i.   Francis Bradley Sr., son of Thomas Bradley and Francis Savile was born in 1625 in Fairfield, Connecticut. He died on 22 Oct 1698 in Fairfield, Connecticut. He married Ruth Barlow. She was born in 1638 in Fairfield, Connecticut. She died on 22 Oct 1689 in Fairfield, Connecticut.

6498. John Barlow was born in 1600 in Manchester, Lancashire, England. He died on 28 Mar 1674 in Fairfield, Connecticut. He married **Ann Ward**.

6499. Ann Ward was born in 1604 in Suffolk, England. She died on 25 Feb 1684 in Fairfield, Connecticut.

Ann Ward and John Barlow had the following child:

    3249.   i.   Ruth Barlow, daughter of John Barlow and Ann Ward was born in 1638 in Fairfield, Connecticut. She died on 22 Oct 1689 in Fairfield, Connecticut. She married Francis Bradley Sr.. He was born in 1625 in Fairfield, Connecticut. He died on 22 Oct 1698 in Fairfield, Connecticut.

6504. Jehu Burr Sr. was born in 1596 in Essex, England. He died in 1671 in Fairfield, Connecticut (Buried at the Old Burying Ground, 430 Beach Road, Fairfield, CT). He married **Elizabeth Cable** in 1624 in En.

6505. Elizabeth Cable was born in 1598 in Essex, England. She died in 1670 in Fairfield, Connecticut.

Elizabeth Cable and Jehu Burr Sr. had the following child:

    3252.   i.   Jehu Burr Jr., son of Jehu Burr Sr. and Elizabeth Cable was born in 1625 in Lavenham, Suffolk, England. He died on 31 Oct 1692 in Fairfield, Connecticut. He married Esther Ward, daughter of Andrew Ward and Hester Sherman on 20 Oct 1658 in Fairfield, Connecticut. She was born in 1623 in Watertown, Middlesex, Massachusetts. She died in 1664 in Fairfield, Connecticut.

6506. Andrew Ward was born in 1597 in Homersfield, Suffolk, England. He died on 28 Feb 1660 in Fairfield, Connecticut. He married **Hester Sherman** in 1627 in England.

6507. Hester Sherman was born on 01 Apr 1606 in Dedham, Essex, England. She died on 28 Feb 1666 in Fairfield, Connecticut.

Hester Sherman and Andrew Ward had the following child:

    3253.   i.   Esther Ward, daughter of Andrew Ward and Hester Sherman was born in 1623 in Watertown, Middlesex, Massachusetts. She died in 1664 in Fairfield, Connecticut. She married Jehu Burr Jr., son of Jehu Burr Sr. and Elizabeth Cable on 20 Oct 1658 in Fairfield, Connecticut. He was born in 1625 in Lavenham, Suffolk, England. He died on 31 Oct 1692 in Fairfield, Connecticut.

6508. Rev. Philip Pinckney, son of William Pynkne and Anna Webb was born in Jan 1584 in Rushall Manor, Rushall, Wiltshire, England. He died in Feb 1658 in Dinton, Wiltshire, England. He married **Margaret Gough** in 1610 in Dinton, Wiltshire, England.

6509. **Margaret Gough** was born in 1591 in Dinton, Wiltshire, England. She died in 1618 in Dinton, Buckinghamshire, England.

Margaret Gough and Rev. Philip Pinckney had the following children:
    i.   Anna Pinckney, daughter of Rev. Philip Pinckney and Margaret Gough was born in 1616 in Dinton, Wiltshire, England.

    ii.   Henrie Pinkney, son of Rev. Philip Pinckney and Margaret Gough was born in 1614 in England. He died in 1678 in England.

    iii.   Bartholomew Pinckney, son of Rev. Philip Pinckney and Margaret Gough was born in 1629 in Dinton, Wiltshire, England. He died on 21 Apr 1659.

    iv.   Dorothy Pinckney, daughter of Rev. Philip Pinckney and Margaret Gough was born in 1635 in Dinton, Wiltshire, England. She died in 1653.

3254.   v.   Phillip Pinckney, son of Rev. Philip Pinckney and Margaret Gough was born on 07 Mar 1618 in Dinton, Wiltshire, England. He died on 28 Feb 1687 in Eastchester, Westchester, New York. He married Jane Phippen, daughter of George Phippen and Joan Rie Penrose on 20 Jun 1648 in Fairfield, Connecticut. She was born in Jan 1629 in England. She died in Feb 1680 in Eastchester, Westchester, New York.

6510. **George Phippen**, son of Robert Phippen and Cecily Jordan was born in 1584 in Melcomb, Dorset, England. He died in Feb 1650 in London, England. He married **Joan Rie Penrose**, daughter of John Penros and Jane Trefusis on 20 Jun 1648 in Weymouth, Dorset, England.

6511. **Joan Rie Penrose**, daughter of John Penros and Jane Trefusis was born in Jan 1589 in Weymouth, Dorset, England. She died in Feb 1650 in England.

Joan Rie Penrose and George Phippen had the following child:
3255.   i.   Jane Phippen, daughter of George Phippen and Joan Rie Penrose was born in Jan 1629 in England. She died in Feb 1680 in Eastchester, Westchester, New York. She married Phillip Pinckney, son of Rev. Philip Pinckney and Margaret Gough on 20 Jun 1648 in Fairfield, Connecticut. He was born on 07 Mar 1618 in Dinton, Wiltshire, England. He died on 28 Feb 1687 in Eastchester, Westchester, New York.

6592. **James Dalrymple**, son of John Dalrymple and Isobel Crawford was born in 1543. He died on 05 Aug 1586.

6593. **Isabel Kennedy**, daughter of Thomas Kennedy and Agnes Montgomerie was born in 1573 in Baltersane, Ayrshire, Scotland.

Isabel Kennedy and James Dalrymple had the following children:
3296.   i.   James Dalrymple, son of James Dalrymple and Isabel Kennedy was born in 1589 in Drummurchie, Barr, Ayrshire, Scotland. He died in Jan 1625 in Barr, Ayrshire, Scotland. She was born in 1598 in Knockdaw, Scotland. She died in 1663 in Scotland.

ii.   John Dalrymple, son of James Dalrymple and Isabel Kennedy was born in 1587 in Scotland.

6594.   Fergus Kennedy, son of David Kennedy Kennedy was born in 1560 in Scotland. He died in 1635 in Knockdaw, Ayrshire, Scotland.

Fergus Kennedy and Euphame McDowell had the following child:
i.   Fergus Kennedy, son of Fergus Kennedy and Euphame McDowell was born in 1590 in Knockdaw, Ayrshire, Scotland. He died in 1643 in Down, Down, Ireland.

Fergus Kennedy had the following child:
3297.   i.   Janet Kennedy, daughter of Fergus Kennedy was born in 1598 in Knockdaw, Scotland. She died in 1663 in Scotland. He was born in 1589 in Drummurchie, Barr, Ayrshire, Scotland. He died in Jan 1625 in Barr, Ayrshire, Scotland.

6596.   Robert Ross, son of James Ross and Jean Sempill was born in 1563 in Renfrewshire, Scotland. He died in Oct 1595 in Renfrewshire, Scotland. He married **Jean Hamilton** in 1591 in Scotland.

6597.   Jean Hamilton was born in 1571 in Ardross, Fife, Scotland. She died in May 1631 in Ardross, Fife, Scotland.

Jean Hamilton and Robert Ross had the following children:
3298.   i.   James Ross, son of Robert Ross and Jean Hamilton was born in 1589 in Hawkhead, Renfrewshire, Scotland. He died on 17 Dec 1633 in Balneil, Wigtownshire, Scotland. He married Sarah Syme in 1613 in Scotland. She was born in 1595. She died in 1623 in Edinburgh, Midlothian, Scotland. He married Margaret Scott on 19 Dec 1614. She was born in 1590 in Buccleuch, Scotland. She died on 03 Oct 1651 in 1652400, Yorkshire, England.
ii.   Jean Ross, daughter of Robert Ross and Jean Hamilton was born in 1590 in Renfrewshire, Scotland. She died in New London, New London, Connecticut, United States.

6600.   Walter Dundas was born in 1580 in Linlithgow, West Lothian, Scotland. He died in 1622 in Fermanagh, Ireland.

6601.   Elizabeth Bruce was born in Linlithgow, West Lothian, Scotland.

Elizabeth Bruce and Walter Dundas had the following child:
3300.   i.   James Dundas, son of Walter Dundas and Elizabeth Bruce was born in 1600 in Magdalens, Scotland. He died in 1637 in Fermanagh, Ireland.

6604.   Thomas Gray was born in 1559 in Barony, Lanarkshire, Scotland. He died in 1671 in Kirkoswald, Ayrshire, Scotland. He married **Margaret Walker**.

6605.   Margaret Walker was born in 1563 in Barony, Lanarkshire, Scotland.

Margaret Walker and Thomas Gray had the following child:
3302.   i.   William Gray, son of Thomas Gray and Margaret Walker was born in 1600 in Pittendrum, Scotland. He died on 04 Aug 1648 in Edinburgh, Midlothian,

Scotland. He married Egidia Smith on 20 Jun 1620 in Midlothian, Scotland. She was born in 1603 in Grothill, Midlothian, Scotland. She died on 17 Sep 1686 in Midlothian, Scotland.

6656. **John Duncan**, son of William Duncan and Agnes Robinson was born in 1530 in Edinburgh, Midlothian, Scotland. He died in 1620 in Perth, Perthshire, Scotland. He married **Jenet Andro**.

6657. **Jenet Andro** was born in 1535 in Edinburgh, Midlothian, Scotland. She died in 1635 in Glasgow, Lanarkshire, Scotland.

Jenet Andro and John Duncan had the following children:

     i.   James Duncan, son of John Duncan and Jenet Andro was born in 1570 in Edinburgh, Midlothian, Scotland.

     ii.   Finlay Duncan, son of John Duncan and Jenet Andro was born in 1561 in Edinburgh, Midlothian, Scotland.

     iii.   John Duncan, son of John Duncan and Jenet Andro was born in 1557 in Edinburgh, Midlothian, Scotland. He died in 1660.

     iv.   Thomas Duncan, son of John Duncan and Jenet Andro was born in 1569 in Edinburgh, Midlothian, Scotland. He died in 1592 in Edinburgh, Midlothian, Scotland.

     v.   Marion Duncan, daughter of John Duncan and Jenet Andro was born in 1563 in Edinburgh, Midlothian, Scotland.

     vi.   Johnne DUNCAN, son of John Duncan and Jenet Andro was born in 1589 in Edinburgh, Midlothian, Scotland. He died in 1650 in Edinburgh, Midlothian, Scotland.

     vii.   John Duncan, son of John Duncan and Jenet Andro was born on 04 May 1600 in Edinburgh, Midlothian, Scotland. He died in 1684 in Dundee, Angus, Scotland.

     viii.   William Duncan, son of John Duncan and Jenet Andro was born on 11 Sep 1601 in Scotland. He died in 1647 in Scotland.

   3328.   ix.   Andrew Duncan, son of John Duncan and Jenet Andro was born in 1575 in Perth, Perthshire, Scotland. He died in 1605 in Dauiot, Aberdeenshire, Scotland. He married Chippewa Indian. She was born in 1580 in United States. She died in 1625 in Scotland.

     x.   Ninian Anderson, son of John Duncan and Jenet Andro was born in 1555 in Dowhill, Stobcross, Scotland. He died in 1630 in Dowhill, Stobcross, Scotland.

7136. **Hans Lang** was born in 1554 in Windlach, Zurich, Switzerland. He died in 1591 in Windlach, Zurich, Switzerland. He married **Elsbeth Baumgartner**.

7137. **Elsbeth Baumgartner** was born in 1556 in Windlach, Zurich, Switzerland. She died in 1591.

Elsbeth Baumgartner and Hans Lang had the following child:

3568.   i.   Hans Lang, son of Hans Lang and Elsbeth Baumgartner was born on 06 Feb 1588 in Windlach, Zurich, Switzerland. He died on 12 Jul 1663 in Windlach, Zurich, Switzerland. He married Margreth Volkhart on 28 Jun 1612 in Stadel Parish, Zurich, Switzerland. She was born in 1591 in Nschikon, Niedechasli, Switzerland. She died on 26 Jan 1651 in Windlach, Zurich, Switzerland.

7140.   **Heinrich Surber** was born in 1571 in Bülach, Zurich, Switzerland. He married **Anna Koch**.

7141.   **Anna Koch** was born in 1575 in Zürich, Zurich, Switzerland.

Anna Koch and Heinrich Surber had the following child:

3570.   i.   Hans Surber, son of Heinrich Surber and Anna Koch was born in 1600 in Switzerland. He died on 21 Aug 1664. He married Elsbeth Kempf. She was born in 1602.

Generation 14

12384.   **Hans Von Tschudi** was born in 1513 in Frenkendorf, Basel-Country, Switzerland. He died in 1538 in Frenkendorf, Basel-Country, Switzerland. He married **Elsa Barth** in 1535 in Basel, Basel Town, Switzerland.

12385.   **Elsa Barth** was born in 1520 in Lausen, Basel, Switzerland. She died in Basel, Basel Town, Switzerland.

Elsa Barth and Hans Von Tschudi had the following child:

6192.   i.   Martin Von Tschudi, son of Hans Von Tschudi and Elsa Barth was born in 1537 in Frenkendorf, Liestal, Basel-Landschaft, Switzerland. He died in Frenkendorf, Liestal, Basel-Landschaft, Switzerland. He married Anna Salatine in 1560 in Frenkendorf, Basel-Country, Switzerland. She was born in 1541 in Frenkendorf, Basel-Country, Switzerland. She died in Basel, Basel-Town, Switzerland.

12420.   **John William De La Marck**, son of William I Duke of Cleves and Maria Habsburg of Austria was born on 28 May 1562. He died on 25 Mar 1609. He married **Anna Van Aldekerk**.

12421.   **Anna Van Aldekerk**.

Anna Van Aldekerk and John William De La Marck had the following child:

6210.   i.   Bishop Herman Isacks Op Den Graeff, son of John William De La Marck and Anna Van Aldekerk was born on 26 Nov 1585 in Aldekerk, Kleve, Nordrhein-Westfalen, Germany. He died on 27 Dec 1642 in Krefeld, Krefeld, Nordrhein-Westfalen, Germany. He married Grietjen Pletjes, daughter of Driessen Andreas Pletjes and Alet Gobels Syllys on 16 Aug 1605 in Kempen, Heinsberg, Nordrhein-Westfalen, Germany. She was born on 26 Nov 1588 in Kempen, Holland. She died on 17 Jan 1642/43 in Krefeld, Krefeld, Nordrhein-Westfalen, Germany.

12422.   **Driessen Andreas Pletjes** was born in 1555 in Kempen, Rheinland, Prussia. He died on 22 May 1608 in Kempen, Rheinland, Prussia. He married **Alet Gobels Syllys** on 13 Dec 1584 in Kempen, Rheinland, Prussia.

12423. **Alet Gobels Syllys** was born in 1563 in Kempen, Rheinland, Prussia. She died in 1615 in Krefeld, Krefeld, Nordrhein-Westfalen, Germany.

Alet Gobels Syllys and Driessen Andreas Pletjes had the following child:

6211.   i.   Grietjen Pletjes, daughter of Driessen Andreas Pletjes and Alet Gobels Syllys was born on 26 Nov 1588 in Kempen, Holland. She died on 17 Jan 1642/43 in Krefeld, Krefeld, Nordrhein-Westfalen, Germany. She married Bishop Herman Isacks Op Den Graeff, son of John William De La Marck and Anna Van Aldekerk on 16 Aug 1605 in Kempen, Heinsberg, Nordrhein-Westfalen, Germany. He was born on 26 Nov 1585 in Aldekerk, Kleve, Nordrhein-Westfalen, Germany. He died on 27 Dec 1642 in Krefeld, Krefeld, Nordrhein-Westfalen, Germany.

13016. **William Pynkne** was born in 1541 in England. He died in 1594 in Rushall, Staffordshire, England. He married **Anna Webb**.

13017. **Anna Webb** was born in 1553 in Lidgate, Suffolk, England. She died in England.

Anna Webb and William Pynkne had the following child:

6508.   i.   Rev. Philip Pinckney, son of William Pynkne and Anna Webb was born in Jan 1584 in Rushall Manor, Rushall, Wiltshire, England. He died in Feb 1658 in Dinton, Wiltshire, England. He married Margaret Gough in 1610 in Dinton, Wiltshire, England. She was born in 1591 in Dinton, Wiltshire, England. She died in 1618 in Dinton, Buckinghamshire, England.

13020. **Robert Phippen** was born in 1555 in Weymouth, Dorset, England. He died on 12 Oct 1589 in Melcombe Regis, Dorset, England. He married **Cecily Jordan**.

13021. **Cecily Jordan** was born in 1559 in Weymouth, Dorset, England. She died in 1603 in Weymouth, Dorset, England.

Cecily Jordan and Robert Phippen had the following child:

6510.   i.   George Phippen, son of Robert Phippen and Cecily Jordan was born in 1584 in Melcomb, Dorset, England. He died in Feb 1650 in London, England. He married Joan Rie Penrose, daughter of John Penros and Jane Trefusis on 20 Jun 1648 in Weymouth, Dorset, England. She was born in Jan 1589 in Weymouth, Dorset, England. She died in Feb 1650 in England.

13022. **John Penros** was born in 1579 in Manaccan, Cornwall, England. He died in England. He married **Jane Trefusis**.

13023. **Jane Trefusis** was born in 1588 in Cornwall, England. She died in 1660.

Jane Trefusis and John Penros had the following child:

6511.   i.   Joan Rie Penrose, daughter of John Penros and Jane Trefusis was born in Jan 1589 in Weymouth, Dorset, England. She died in Feb 1650 in England. She married George Phippen, son of Robert Phippen and Cecily Jordan on 20 Jun 1648 in Weymouth, Dorset, England. He was born in 1584 in Melcomb, Dorset, England. He died in Feb 1650 in London, England.

13184. **John Dalrymple**, son of William Dalrymple and Margaret Wallace was born in 1544.

13185. Isobel Crawford.

Isobel Crawford and John Dalrymple had the following child:
6592. i. James Dalrymple, son of John Dalrymple and Isobel Crawford was born in 1543. He died on 05 Aug 1586. She was born in 1573 in Baltersane, Ayrshire, Scotland.

13186. Thomas Kennedy was born in 1534 in Bargany, Ayrshire, Scotland. He died in 1597.

13187. Agnes Montgomerie was born in 1541 in Cunninghame, Ayrshire, Scotland. She died in Bargany, Ayrshire, Scotland.

Agnes Montgomerie and Thomas Kennedy had the following child:
6593. i. Isabel Kennedy, daughter of Thomas Kennedy and Agnes Montgomerie was born in 1573 in Baltersane, Ayrshire, Scotland. He was born in 1543. He died on 05 Aug 1586.

13188. David Kennedy Kennedy was born in 1520 in Maybole, Ayrshire, Scotland. He died in 1582 in Knockdaw, Ayrshire, Scotland.

David Kennedy Kennedy had the following child:
6594. i. Fergus Kennedy, son of David Kennedy Kennedy was born in 1560 in Scotland. He died in 1635 in Knockdaw, Ayrshire, Scotland. He married Euphame McDowell. She died in Knockdaw, Ayrshire, Scotland.

13192. James Ross was born in 1517 in Renfrewshire, Scotland. He died on 02 Apr 1581 in Renfrewshire, Scotland. He married **Jean Sempill**.

13193. Jean Sempill was born in 1543 in Renfrew, Renfrewshire, Scotland. She died on 28 Feb 1592 in Hawkhead, Renfrewshire, Scotland.

Jean Sempill and James Ross had the following child:
6596. i. Robert Ross, son of James Ross and Jean Sempill was born in 1563 in Renfrewshire, Scotland. He died in Oct 1595 in Renfrewshire, Scotland. He married Jean Hamilton in 1591 in Scotland. She was born in 1571 in Ardross, Fife, Scotland. She died in May 1631 in Ardross, Fife, Scotland.

13312. William Duncan, son of Allan Duncan and Jonat Crosby was born in 1501 in Dunfermline, Fife, Scotland. He died on 27 May 1574 in Paisley, Renfrewshire, Scotland. He married **Agnes Robinson**.

13313. Agnes Robinson, daughter of George Robinson was born in 1509 in Dunfermline, Fife, Scotland. She died in 1597 in Scotland.

Agnes Robinson and William Duncan had the following children:
6656. i. John Duncan, son of William Duncan and Agnes Robinson was born in 1530 in Edinburgh, Midlothian, Scotland. He died in 1620 in Perth, Perthshire, Scotland. He married Jenet Andro. She was born in 1535 in Edinburgh, Midlothian, Scotland. She died in 1635 in Glasgow, Lanarkshire, Scotland.

       ii. John Duncan, son of William Duncan and Agnes Robinson was born in 1531 in Pitochry, Scotland. He died in 1590 in Perthsire, Scotland.

24840. **William I Duke of Cleves**, son of John III Duke of Cleves and Maria of Julich-Berg was born on 18 Jul 1516 in Dusseldorf, Nordrhein-Westfalen, Germany. He died on 05 Jan 1592 in Dusseldorf, Nordrhein-Westfalen, Germany. He married **Maria Habsburg of Austria**.

24841. **Maria Habsburg of Austria**, daughter of Ferdinand I Holy Roman Emperor and Anna of Bohemia and Hungary was born on 15 May 1531 in Wien, Vienna, Austria. She died on 11 Dec 1581 in Hambach, Duren, Nordrhein-Westfalen, Germany.

Maria Habsburg of Austria and William I Duke of Cleves had the following child:

12420. i. John William De La Marck, son of William I Duke of Cleves and Maria Habsburg of Austria was born on 28 May 1562. He died on 25 Mar 1609. He married Anna Van Aldekerk.

26368. **William Dalrymple**, son of William Dalrymple and Marion Chalmers was born in 1530. He married **Margaret Wallace**.

26369. **Margaret Wallace** was born in Trabzon, Turkey.

Margaret Wallace and William Dalrymple had the following child:

13184. i. John Dalrymple, son of William Dalrymple and Margaret Wallace was born in 1544.

26624. **Allan Duncan** was born in 1460 in Garbred, Fife, Scotland. He died on 27 May 1574 in Scotland. He married **Jonat Crosby**.

26625. **Jonat Crosby** was born in 1460 in Garbred, Scotland. She died in Scotland.

Jonat Crosby and Allan Duncan had the following child:

13312. i. William Duncan, son of Allan Duncan and Jonat Crosby was born in 1501 in Dunfermline, Fife, Scotland. He died on 27 May 1574 in Paisley, Renfrewshire, Scotland. He married Agnes Robinson. She was born in 1509 in Dunfermline, Fife, Scotland. She died in 1597 in Scotland.

26626. **George Robinson** was born in 1460 in Govan, Lanarkshire, Scotland. He died in 1550 in Govan, Lanarkshire, Scotland.

George Robinson had the following child:

13313. i. Agnes Robinson, daughter of George Robinson was born in 1509 in Dunfermline, Fife, Scotland. She died in 1597 in Scotland. She married William Duncan. He was born in 1501 in Dunfermline, Fife, Scotland. He died on 27 May 1574 in Paisley, Renfrewshire, Scotland.

49680. **John III Duke of Cleves**, son of John II Duke of Cleves and Mathilde of Hesse was born on 10 Nov 1490. He died on 06 Feb 1538. He married **Maria of Julich-Berg**.

49681. **Maria of Julich-Berg**, daughter of William IV Duke of Julich-Berg was born on 03 Aug 1491 in Jülich, Duren, Nordrhein-Westfalen, Germany. She died on 29 Aug 1543.

Maria of Julich-Berg and John III Duke of Cleves had the following child:

24840. i.   William I Duke of Cleves, son of John III Duke of Cleves and Maria of Julich-Berg
                was born on 18 Jul 1516 in Dusseldorf, Nordrhein-Westfalen, Germany. He died
                on 05 Jan 1592 in Dusseldorf, Nordrhein-Westfalen, Germany. He married Maria
                Habsburg of Austria. She was born on 15 May 1531 in Wien, Vienna, Austria. She
                died on 11 Dec 1581 in Hambach, Duren, Nordrhein-Westfalen, Germany.

49682. **Ferdinand I Holy Roman Emperor**, son of Philip Habsburg I of Castile and Joanna
        Juana La Loca Trastamara was born on 10 Mar 1503 in Alcalá de Henares, Madrid,
        Madrid, Spain. He died on 25 Jul 1564 in Vienna, Austria. He married **Anna of
        Bohemia and Hungary**.

49683. **Anna of Bohemia and Hungary** was born on 23 Jul 1503 in Praha, Czech Republic.
        She died on 27 Jan 1547 in Praha, Czech Republic.

Anna of Bohemia and Hungary and Ferdinand I Holy Roman Emperor had the following
children:

        i.   Elisabeth Archduchess of Austria, daughter of Ferdinand I Holy Roman Emperor
                and Anna of Bohemia and Hungary was born on 09 Jun 1526 in Linz, Linz, Upper
                Austria, Austria. She died on 15 Jun 1545 in Poland.

        ii.   Helen Austria, daughter of Ferdinand I Holy Roman Emperor and Anna of
                Bohemia and Hungary was born on 07 Jan 1543 in Wien, Wien, Vienna, Austria.
                She died on 05 Mar 1574.

        iii.   Ursule Archduchess Austria, daughter of Ferdinand I Holy Roman Emperor and
                Anna of Bohemia and Hungary was born on 24 Jul 1541 in Wien, Wien, Vienna,
                Austria. She died on 30 Apr 1543.

        iv.   Charles II Archduke of Austria, son of Ferdinand I Holy Roman Emperor and Anna
                of Bohemia and Hungary was born on 03 Jun 1540 in Wien, Wien, Vienna,
                Austria. He died on 10 Jul 1590 in Graz, Graz, Styria, Austria.

        v.   Johann Archduke Austria, son of Ferdinand I Holy Roman Emperor and Anna of
                Bohemia and Hungary was born on 10 Apr 1538 in Wien, Wien, Vienna, Austria.
                He died on 20 Mar 1539.

        vi.   Johanna of Austria, daughter of Ferdinand I Holy Roman Emperor and Anna of
                Bohemia and Hungary was born on 24 Jan 1547 in Praha, Praha, Czech Republic.
                She died on 10 Apr 1578 in Florence Italian Firenze is the capital, Italy.

        vii.   Eleanor Austria, daughter of Ferdinand I Holy Roman Emperor and Anna of
                Bohemia and Hungary was born on 02 Nov 1534 in Wien, Wien, Vienna, Austria.
                She died on 05 Aug 1594 in Mantua, Mantova, Lombardia, Italy.

        viii.   Catharine Archduchess Austria, daughter of Ferdinand I Holy Roman Emperor
                and Anna of Bohemia and Hungary was born on 15 Sep 1533 in Innsbruck,
                Innsbruck-Stadt, Tyrol, Austria. She died on 28 Feb 1572 in Linz, Linz, Upper

Austria, Austria.

   ix.   Magdalene Archduchess Austria, daughter of Ferdinand I Holy Roman Emperor and Anna of Bohemia and Hungary was born on 14 Aug 1532 in Innsbruck, Innsbruck-Stadt, Tyrol, Austria. She died on 10 Sep 1590.

   x.   Ferdinand Archduke Of Austria, son of Ferdinand I Holy Roman Emperor and Anna of Bohemia and Hungary was born on 14 Jun 1529 in Linz, Linz, Upper Austria, Austria. He died on 24 Jan 1595 in Innsbruck, Innsbruck-Stadt, Tyrol, Austria.

   xi.   Anna of Austria, daughter of Ferdinand I Holy Roman Emperor and Anna of Bohemia and Hungary was born on 07 Jul 1528 in Wien, Wien, Vienna, Austria. She died on 16 Oct 1590 in Mhunchen, Oberbayern, Bayern, Germany.

   xii.   Maximilian, son of Ferdinand I Holy Roman Emperor and Anna of Bohemia and Hungary was born on 31 Jul 1527 in Wien, Vienna, Austria. He died on 12 Oct 1576 in Regensburg, Bavaria, Prussia, Germany.

   xiii.   Margarethe Archduchess Austria, daughter of Ferdinand I Holy Roman Emperor and Anna of Bohemia and Hungary was born on 16 Feb 1536 in Wien, Wien, Vienna, Austria. She died on 12 Mar 1567.

24841.   xiv.   Maria Habsburg of Austria, daughter of Ferdinand I Holy Roman Emperor and Anna of Bohemia and Hungary was born on 15 May 1531 in Wien, Vienna, Austria. She died on 11 Dec 1581 in Hambach, Duren, Nordrhein-Westfalen, Germany. She married William I Duke of Cleves. He was born on 18 Jul 1516 in Dusseldorf, Nordrhein-Westfalen, Germany. He died on 05 Jan 1592 in Dusseldorf, Nordrhein-Westfalen, Germany.

52736. **William Dalrymple**, son of William Dalrymple and Agnes Kennedy was born in 1494. He married **Marion Chalmers**.

52737. **Marion Chalmers**.

Marion Chalmers and William Dalrymple had the following child:

26368. i.   William Dalrymple, son of William Dalrymple and Marion Chalmers was born in 1530. He married Margaret Wallace. She was born in Trabzon, Turkey.

Generation 17

99360. **John II Duke of Cleves**, son of John I Duke of Cleves and Elizabeth Of Nevers was born in 1458 in Bruxelles, Brabant, Belgium. He died in 1521 in Cleve, Gutersloh, Nordrhein-Westfalen, Germany. He married **Mathilde of Hesse**.

99361. **Mathilde of Hesse** was born on 04 Jul 1473 in Blankenstein, Ennepe-Ruhr-Kreis, Nordrhein-Westfalen, Germany. She died on 19 Feb 1505 in Oder, Brandenburg, Germany (Frankfurt).

Mathilde of Hesse and John II Duke of Cleves had the following child:

49680. i. John III Duke of Cleves, son of John II Duke of Cleves and Mathilde of Hesse was born on 10 Nov 1490. He died on 06 Feb 1538. He married Maria of Julich-Berg. She was born on 03 Aug 1491 in Jülich, Duren, Nordrhein-Westfalen, Germany. She died on 29 Aug 1543.

99362. **William IV Duke of Julich-Berg**, son of Gerhard VII Duke of Julich-Berg was born on 09 Jan 1455. He died on 06 Sep 1511.

William IV Duke of Julich-Berg had the following child:

49681. i. Maria of Julich-Berg, daughter of William IV Duke of Julich-Berg was born on 03 Aug 1491 in Jülich, Duren, Nordrhein-Westfalen, Germany. She died on 29 Aug 1543. She married John III Duke of Cleves. He was born on 10 Nov 1490. He died on 06 Feb 1538.

99364. **Philip Habsburg I of Castile**, son of Maximilian I Holy Roman Emperor was born on 22 Jul 1478 in Bruges, Gironde, Aquitaine, France. He died on 25 Sep 1506 in Burgos, Burgos, Castilla-Leon, Spain. He married **Joanna Juana La Loca Trastamara**.

99365. **Joanna Juana La Loca Trastamara** was born on 06 Nov 1479 in Toledo, Toledo, Castilla-La Mancha, Spain. She died on 13 Apr 1555 in Tordesillas, Valladolid, Castilla-Leon, Spain.

Joanna Juana La Loca Trastamara and Philip Habsburg I of Castile had the following child:

49682. i. Ferdinand I Holy Roman Emperor, son of Philip Habsburg I of Castile and Joanna Juana La Loca Trastamara was born on 10 Mar 1503 in Alcalá de Henares, Madrid, Madrid, Spain. He died on 25 Jul 1564 in Vienna, Austria. He married Anna of Bohemia and Hungary. She was born on 23 Jul 1503 in Praha, Czech Republic. She died on 27 Jan 1547 in Praha, Czech Republic.

105472. **William Dalrymple** was born about 1450. He married **Agnes Kennedy**.

105473. **Agnes Kennedy** was born in 1425 in Stair, Ayrshire, Scotland.

Agnes Kennedy and William Dalrymple had the following child:

52736. i. William Dalrymple, son of William Dalrymple and Agnes Kennedy was born in 1494. He married Marion Chalmers.

Generation 18

198720. **John I Duke of Cleves**, son of Adolph I Duke of Cleves and Marie of Burgundy Duchess of Cleves was born on 16 Feb 1419. He died on 05 Sep 1481. He married **Elizabeth Of Nevers**.

198721. **Elizabeth Of Nevers** was born in 1439 in Nevers, Nievre, Bourgogne, France. She died in 1483 in Kleef, Mettmann, Nordrhein-Westfalen, Germany.

Elizabeth Of Nevers and John I Duke of Cleves had the following child:

99360. i. John II Duke of Cleves, son of John I Duke of Cleves and Elizabeth Of Nevers was born in 1458 in Bruxelles, Brabant, Belgium. He died in 1521 in Cleve, Gutersloh, Nordrhein-Westfalen, Germany. He married Mathilde Of Hesse in 1490. She was born in 1473 in Nassau, Deggendorf, Bayern, Germany. She died in 1505 in Köln,

Koln, Nordrhein-Westfalen, Germany. He married Mathilde of Hesse. She was
born on 04 Jul 1473 in Blankenstein, Ennepe-Ruhr-Kreis, Nordrhein-Westfalen,
Germany. She died on 19 Feb 1505 in Oder, Brandenburg, Germany (Frankfurt).

198724. Gerhard VII Duke of Julich-Berg was born in 1416. He died on 19 Aug 1475.

Gerhard VII Duke of Julich-Berg had the following child:

99362. i.   William IV Duke of Julich-Berg, son of Gerhard VII Duke of Julich-Berg was born
on 09 Jan 1455. He died on 06 Sep 1511.

198728. Maximilian I Holy Roman Emperor, son of Frederick III Holy Roman Emperor was
born on 22 Mar 1459. He died on 12 Jan 1519.

Maximilian I Holy Roman Emperor had the following child:

99364. i.   Philip Habsburg I of Castile, son of Maximilian I Holy Roman Emperor was born
on 22 Jul 1478 in Bruges, Gironde, Aquitaine, France. He died on 25 Sep 1506 in
Burgos, Burgos, Castilla-Leon, Spain. He married Joanna Juana La Loca
Trastamara. She was born on 06 Nov 1479 in Toledo, Toledo, Castilla-La
Mancha, Spain. She died on 13 Apr 1555 in Tordesillas, Valladolid, Castilla-Leon,
Spain.

Generation 19

397440. Adolph I Duke of Cleves, son of Adolph III Duke of Cleves and Margaret of Julich was
born on 02 Aug 1373. He died on 23 Sep 1448. He married **Marie of Burgundy
Duchess of Cleves** on 22 Jul 1406 in Dijon, Cote d'Or, Bourgogne, France.

397441. Marie of Burgundy Duchess of Cleves was born in 1393 in Dijon, Cantal, Auvergne,
France. She died on 30 Oct 1463 in Kalkar, Euskirchen, Nordrhein-Westfalen,
Germany.

Marie of Burgundy Duchess of Cleves and Adolph I Duke of Cleves had the following child:

198720. i.   John I Duke of Cleves, son of Adolph I Duke of Cleves and Marie of Burgundy
Duchess of Cleves was born on 16 Feb 1419. He died on 05 Sep 1481. He married
Elizabeth Of Nevers. She was born in 1439 in Nevers, Nievre, Bourgogne,
France. She died in 1483 in Kleef, Mettmann, Nordrhein-Westfalen, Germany.

397456. Frederick III Holy Roman Emperor was born on 21 Sep 1415. He died on 19 Aug
1493.

Frederick III Holy Roman Emperor had the following child:

198728. i.   Maximilian I Holy Roman Emperor, son of Frederick III Holy Roman Emperor was
born on 22 Mar 1459. He died on 12 Jan 1519.

Generation 20

794880. Adolph III Duke of Cleves, son of Adolph II Count of Marck and Margaret of Cleves
was born in 1334. He died on 07 Sep 1394 in Heiligenstadt, Altotting, Bayern,
Germany. He married **Margaret of Julich** in 1369.

794881. Margaret of Julich was born in 1342 in Amberg, Amberg, Bayern, Germany. She died
in 1425 in Kleve, Rheinland-Pfalz, Germany.

Margaret of Julich and Adolph III Duke of Cleves had the following child:

397440. i. Adolph I Duke of Cleves, son of Adolph III Duke of Cleves and Margaret of Julich was born on 02 Aug 1373. He died on 23 Sep 1448. He married Marie of Burgundy Duchess of Cleves on 22 Jul 1406 in Dijon, Cote d'Or, Bourgogne, France. She was born in 1393 in Dijon, Cantal, Auvergne, France. She died on 30 Oct 1463 in Kalkar, Euskirchen, Nordrhein-Westfalen, Germany.

www.ingramcontent.com/pod-product-compliance
Lightning Source LLC
Chambersburg PA
CBHW080258030726
47593CB00009B/2538